WOMEN
in Ministry
...in God's Service

Dirk Waren

Soaring Eagle Press

WOMEN in Ministry …in God's Service

Unless otherwise indicated, all Scripture quotations are taken from the Holy Bible, New International Version®. NIV®. Copyright © 1973, 1978, 1984, 2011 by the International Bible Society. Used by permission of Zondervan Bible Publishers.

Other translations are listed in the Bibliography.

All underlining, italics and bracketed notes in scriptural citations are added by the author.

Pronominal references to Deity in this work are not always capitalized.

Edited by KEEII; special thanks to Raquel J. ("Sarita") for motivation.

The cover photo is of Jennifer Waren on the California coast.

ISBN: 978-0-578-92356-7
PUBLISHED BY SOARING EAGLE PRESS
Youngstown

Printed in the United States of America

There is neither Jew nor Greek, there is neither slave nor free, there is no male and female, for you are all one in Christ Jesus.

- Galatians 3:28

CONTENTS

1

Women, the Genesis Curse and Emancipation in Christ

'Ministry' means "service" and 'minister' means "servant" (Matthew 20:25-28). As such, the women who functioned in God's service in one capacity or another in the Bible were **women in ministry**. In this book we're going to look at these women and what they did for the LORD.

Of course one of the main questions we want to tackle is whether or not women can serve in positions of ministry in the body of Christ, including the fivefold ministry, that is, serve as apostles, prophets, evangelists, pastors or teachers (Ephesians 4:11-13).

An understandable response is: Why *can't* woman serve in ministry and be ministers? After all, were Aimee Semple McPherson and Kathryn Kuhlman in gross sin by serving as healing evangelists, reaching millions in the 20th Century? (That's a rhetorical question).

The reason this topic is important is because there are sincere believers in the body of Christ who question the legitimacy of women in ministry and base their disapproval (or, at least, agnosticism) mostly on a couple verses in the New Testament. We'll honestly examine those verses, but we're going to first lay some vital groundwork in this chapter and then examine the myriad notable women in the Bible, both New Testament and Old Testament. However, if you want to go straight to the two supposed "hard sayings" on women in the New Testament, just jump ahead to chapters **5** and **6**.

Now let's start with some foundational passages on the topic...

Understanding the "Genesis Curse"

Christ came to set people free from the bondage of sin & death, which includes its expression in human relationships. For instance, Paul taught by the Spirit: "There is neither Jew nor Greek, there is neither slave nor free, **there is no male and female**, **for you are all one in Christ Jesus**." (Galatians 3:28 ESV). We'll look at this text closer in the next section; let's first go back to the very beginning of humanity after Adam & Eve sinned to establish some fundamental points...

> **14 So the Lord God said to the serpent, "Because you have done this,**
>
> **"Cursed are you above all livestock**
>   **and all wild animals!**
>   **You will crawl on your belly**
>   **and you will eat dust**
>   **all the days of your life.**
> **15 And I will put enmity**

<u>between you and the woman,</u>
  <u>and between your offspring and hers;</u>
 he will crush your head,
  and you will strike his heel."

[16] To the woman he said,

"I will make your pains in childbearing very severe;
  with painful labor you will give birth to children.
 <u>Your desire will be for your husband,</u>
  <u>and he will rule over you.</u>"

[17] To Adam he said, "Because you listened to your wife and ate fruit from the tree about which I commanded you, 'You must not eat from it,'

"Cursed is the ground because of you;
   through painful toil you will eat food from it
   all the days of your life.
[18] It will produce thorns and thistles for you,
   and you will eat the plants of the field.
[19] By the sweat of your brow
   you will eat your food
  until you return to the ground,
   since from it you were taken;
  for dust you are
   and to dust you will return."

[20] Adam named his wife Eve, because she would become the mother of all the living.

Genesis 3:14-20

When God pronounced to Eve that "Your desire will be for your husband, **and he will rule over you**" (verse 16) the Creator *was issuing a warning to Eve, not giving a command to Adam.* In other words, God was *not* giving Adam (and men in general) permission to be tyrants over the women in their lives. The LORD was basically saying: "Beware, Eve, man is now going to try to dominate you and your female descendants." This tendency is in the flesh of all males. You can even see it in boys who naturally try to dominate their mothers (which they generally don't do with their fathers, and wisely so). I know because I myself did this when I was a kid. Don't mistake what I'm saying, the masculine spirit is good — God called it "very good" along with everything else that was created (Genesis 1:31) — but the flesh, the sinful nature, perverts all good things.

We must understand that this section of Scripture — Genesis 3:14-19 — is a divine proclamation concerning the **result of** humanity now being fallen. In other words it was a prophetic *curse* due to transgression, **not** a blessing or command, which is why this part of Scripture is called "the Genesis curse." Nothing in this proclamation is a moral law like "You shall not commit adultery" or "You shall not steal" (Exodus 20:14-15), rather it's a divine judgment — a curse — on the serpent/satan for deception and on Adam & Eve for their sin. The only sense that any proclamation in Genesis 3:14-19 is "Law" is that it's contained in the section of Scripture known as the Law or Pentateuch, aka the first five books of the Bible. The fact that some ministers refer to Genesis 3:16 as "Law" or a "blessing" is laughable. I can't help but suspect they have issues with misogyny.

Since humanity has the potential for redemption whereas satan is incorrigible, we're going to focus on the LORD's proclamation to Adam & Eve. God was conveying the general way it will be for them & their progeny — humanity — in a fallen world, not the way it *should* be or *has* to be. For instance…

- The LORD said to Eve that he would "sharply increase your pain in childbirth," but this doesn't mean that a woman and those who are assisting her medically shouldn't do everything in their power to ease her pain during childbirth.
- The LORD said "in pain you will bring forth children," but this doesn't mean that a woman *has* to have children or *will* have children. What about women who can't find a husband? What about women who have no interest in having sex with men? What about women who want to forsake marriage & children in order to devote their lives to God à la 1 Corinthians 7:34? What about women who *can't* have children for one reason or another? What about women who simply have no desire to bear & raise children?
- The LORD said "Your desire will be for your husband," but this clearly doesn't mean *every* woman will desire a husband.
- The LORD said "and he will rule over you," but this doesn't mean he *ought* to rule over her (more on this momentarily).
- The LORD said to Adam "cursed is the ground because of you; through toil you will eat of it all the days of your life," but this doesn't mean that we *shouldn't* improve agriculture quality and production, nor does it mean that people since that time *have* to limit their diet to fruits & vegetables.
- The LORD said "through toil you will eat," but this doesn't mean that we shouldn't reduce the amount of needless toil in our work in order to make a living. The biblical book of wisdom says "The blessing of the LORD brings wealth, without painful toil for it" (Proverbs 10:22).

- The LORD said "By the sweat of your brow you will eat your bread," but this doesn't mean that we shouldn't find ways to reduce the amount of sweat it takes to earn a living.
- Lastly, the LORD said in the latter part of verse 19 that death is now a reality for humanity obviously because "the wages of sin is death," but this doesn't mean that there aren't exceptions to suffering physical death, like Enoch (Genesis 5:21-24), Elijah (2 Kings 2:11) and those who will be raptured (1 Thessalonians 4:13-18). Nor does it mean we shouldn't reconcile with God through the message of Christ to escape eternal death (Romans 6:23 & John 3:16).

In short, these statements are general truths about the way life will be in a fallen world due to Adam & Eve's sin — called "original sin" by theologians — but **they are not absolutes nor are they moral laws or blessings**. They warn of the way it will generally be in this cursed physical reality, but not the way it *should* be or *has* to be or *always will* be. Are you following?

There are two elements of the Genesis Curse that apply to our topic:

1. The statement in verse 16 that the husband will "rule over" the wife reveals that tyrannical gender hierarchy is a *result of* the corruption of sin in a fallen world. God was warning that the male will have a fleshly tendency to dominate his female mate, which can be attributed to his generally larger mass & muscle, as well as a typically more aggressive mentality (which happened to be a good thing back in the day when barbarians threatened the country or homestead). In other words, because the male is generally bigger, stronger and more aggressive he will be inclined to carnally control the female in their relationship; that is, "rule over" her.

2. The other is God's statement to the devil (who possessed the serpent in order to deceive Eve): "I will put enmity between you and the woman" (Genesis 3:15). This shows that **there is enmity between satan and women** because the Messiah, the destroyer of the devil's work, would ultimately come through a woman (Hebrews 2:14 & 1 John 3:8). Satan hates all humankind, of course, but he especially hates women for this reason; in short, **satan is the ultimate misogynist**. This explains why throughout history the devil has moved upon males to subjugate women, which can be observed in societies around the globe ever since. Look no further than strict Muslim countries today and the underground slave market. Even in liberated Western countries, like the USA, women didn't get the right to vote until 1920!

Yet God does *not* want the male to "rule over" his mate nor males to "rule over" women in general in any type of abusively domineering sense. This is clearly observed in both the Old and New Testaments.

For instance, Ephesians 5:25 shows that the leadership of the husband in the marriage is to be *loving* and *self-sacrificial* in nature, *not* domineering; in fact, husbands are to love their wives **in the sense of Christ loving the Church and giving up his life for it**. The Greek word for 'love' in this verse refers to *practical* love, not a feeling. It is defined in the famous love passage 1 Corinthians 13:4-7. If husbands make it a point to practice this kind of love 99% of wives would *gladly* acquiesce if there's a disagreement.

You could say that Ephesians 5:25 *counteracts* the curse of Genesis 3:16. Other New Testament verses do the same thing, like Ephesians 5:28, Colossians 3:19 and 1 Peter 3:7. God is basically saying to husbands: "Your flesh naturally wants to dominate your wife; I'm instructing you to *love* her and *honor* her as your own body in a self-sacrificial manner."

Another vital point to keep in mind is that the husband having headship in the marriage **does not mean inequality or superiority** because 1 Corinthians 11:3 parallels the husband's headship over the wife with God's headship over Christ. Are the Father and Son equal? Of course they are. Jesus said "I and the Father are one" (John 10:30). Similarly, husbands and wives are supposed to be *one* ideally (Matthew 19:4-6 & Ephesians 5:31).

Whilst Father and Son are equally the LORD, Yahweh (Genesis 1:26 & John 1:1-3), there is subordination in an economical, relational sense. For instance, the Scriptures very clearly show that the Father is the head over the Son and this is explicitly stated (1 Corinthians 11:3 & 15:27-28). Although the Father and Son are equal in being, the Son is subordinate to the Father in function or relationship. This is paralleled to the relationship of husbands and wives.

Furthermore, God gave *both* Adam & Eve the commission to subdue or govern the Earth, not just Adam (Genesis 1:28). This suggests equality and teamwork, not one being superior to the other. We'll look at this further in chapter 7.

It should be noted that the same Greek word for 'submit' used in the context of wives submitting to their husbands (Colossians 3:18) **is also used in reference to believers submitting "to one another out of reverence for Christ," which illustrates a spirit of *mutual* submission** (Ephesians 5:21-25). This means we should strive to get along and give preference to one another. I'm pointing this out so you plainly see that submitting to others in a spirit of humility is a universal concept in the body of Christ — for males and females

— and not just something wives are to exclusively do with their husbands.

In regards to the Old Testament, notice what the LORD commanded concerning newlyweds:

> **If a man has recently married, he must not be sent to war or have any other duty laid on him. For one year he is to be free to stay at home <u>and bring happiness to the wife he has married</u>.**
> **Deuteronomy 24:5**

God is so concerned about marriages being healthy and starting off on the right foot that newlywed husbands in Israel were *not* permitted to go to war for a full year or be burdened by any other duty so that they could stay home and **bring happiness to their wives!** Moreover, the book of wisdom says that the Earth figuratively trembles at the very idea of a married woman being *unloved* (Proverbs 30:21-23). Does this remotely sound like the LORD wants the husband to "rule over" the wife? Obviously not. God wants husbands to **love their wives and bring happiness to them!**

Or consider Abraham, the progenitor of the Israelites and our "father of faith" (Romans 4). Did he "rule over" his wife Sarah (who was originally named Sarai)? It was Sarah who made the decision to give her servant, Hagar, to Abraham so that he could have children through her since Sarah couldn't bear offspring at the time (Genesis 16). It was also Sarah's decision to exile Hagar & Ishmael (the latter being Abraham & Hagar's child) after she became jealous. While these decisions may have been dubious, **Abraham complied with both** (Genesis 21). This shows that Sarah had the freedom in their relationship to make life-changing decisions in the domestic realm and Abraham willingly abided by them. Clearly, Abraham didn't "rule over" Sarah.

This corresponds to Paul's instructions in 1 Timothy 5:14 where he said wives are "to manage their homes." This phrase is one compound word in the Greek, *oikodespoteó (oy-kod-es-pot-EH-oh)*, which means "to rule the household." This suggests that, while the husband is the head of the marriage, the wife is the domestic head.

For irrefutable proof that the Genesis curse did *not* mean males were to rule over women in general, the LORD chose & anointed Deborah **to lead Israel *spiritually*, *legally* and *militarily* for 40 years** (Judges 4:4-9). God selected Deborah to fulfill this great leadership position in a generally patriarchal region of the globe. Why? Obviously because she was qualified for the job above any male. The most qualified man, Barak, wouldn't even go to battle without her presence! We'll look at Deborah in more detail next chapter.

Christianity Destroys the Idea that We are Inferior due to Race, Status or Gender

The message of Christ is the 'gospel' — literally the "Good News" — because those who believe are regenerated (Titus 3:5) and become "new creations" (2 Corinthians 5:17) **free from bondage to sin & death**, which would include its expression in human relationships — discrimination due to race, social status or gender:

> **So in Christ Jesus you are all children of God through faith, [27] for all of you who were baptized into Christ have clothed yourselves with Christ. [28] There is <u>neither Jew nor Gentile, neither slave nor free, nor is there male and female</u>, for <u>you are all one in Christ Jesus</u>.**
>
> **Galatians 3:26-28**

Paul's letter to the Galatian assemblies is one of the earliest epistles of the New Covenant and **establishes** something **foundational**: "There is neither Jew nor Greek, there is neither slave nor free, there is no male and female, for you are all one in Christ Jesus" (ESV). This passage does not *deny* the existence in this fallen world of different races, social statuses or the two genders, but rather points out that *in* Christ Jesus — that is, in covenant (contract) with God thru Christ — we are all one body. While all believers are at different levels of spiritual growth and have different gifting or offices, we "are all one in Christ Jesus." This explains why the Messiah taught against the practice of titles for leaders in the Church and emphasized the **equalitarian nature** of leadership (Matthew 23:7-11). Certainly the Scriptures acknowledge servant-oriented leadership in the kingdom of God — that is, leadership *positions* or *offices* and the gifting necessary for such (Ephesians 4:11) — but personal titles are a different story. Christ emphasized that believers "are all brothers and sisters."[1]

There is no male or female in Christ. As such, women are free to learn in the assemblies and serve in ministry; that is, **participate in God's service**. While this is true, Christians have to be sensitive to the customs of the region in which they are ministering if they want to effectively reach the people thereof. If they introduce ideas

---

[1] The example set for us in the blueprint of Holy Scripture is that Paul was just called "Paul" (2 Peter 3:15) and other great fivefold ministers were simply called by name as well (Galatians 2:6-9).

that are too radical to the area's established mores it'll give Christianity & the gospel a bad rap and hinder the chances of reaching the inhabitants. This is why it's necessary to "become all things to all people so that by all possible means [we] might save some," as Paul put it (1 Corinthians 9:19-23).

We'll look at some of these things in greater detail as we continue, let's now consider…

2

Women in Ministry in the New Testament

The New Testament cites myriad women involved in serving God in one capacity or another. Let's begin with…

Priscilla

Priscilla and her husband, Aquila, came from Italy to Corinth after the Emperor Claudius expelled Hebrews from Rome via executive order. They were tentmakers who met Paul in Corinth (Acts 18:2) and eventually traveled with him to Ephesus, which is where Paul's protégé, Timothy, later served as a pastor (Acts 18:18-19 & 2 Timothy 4:19). A small church — a Christian assembly — regularly met **in Priscilla & Aquila's house** (1 Corinthians 16:19). Notice what Paul says about this couple in his letter to Roman believers:

> Greet **Priscilla and Aquila, my co-workers in Christ Jesus.** [4] They risked their lives for me. Not only I but all the churches of the Gentiles are grateful to them.
> [5] Greet also the church that meets at their house.
>
> **Romans 16:3-5**

This reveals that Priscilla & Aquila served the Gentile churches. Note how Paul mentions Priscilla *before* Aquila and acknowledges both as "**my co-workers** in Christ Jesus." While Paul was obviously in charge as he was the most prominent apostle of the New Testament, he referred to these two fellow servants in an equalitarian sense even though they were technically *under* him in the Church. This corresponds to what was noted at the end of the last chapter — believers "are all one in Christ Jesus," whether Jew or Gentile, slave or free, male or female (Galatians 3:28), and servant-leadership in the Church is *equalitarian* in nature (Matthew 23:7-11).

Now notice what took place in Ephesus after Priscilla & Aquila heard a mighty man of God speak at the local synagogue:

> **Meanwhile, a Jew named Apollos, a native of Alexandria, came to Ephesus. He was a learned man, with a thorough knowledge of the Scriptures.** [25] **He had been instructed in the way of the Lord, and he spoke with great fervor and taught about Jesus accurately, though he knew only the baptism of John.** [26] **He began to speak boldly in the synagogue. When Priscilla and Aquila heard him, they invited him to their home and explained to him the way of God more adequately.**
>
> **Acts 18:24-26**

Once again, Priscilla is mentioned *before* Aquila, and this time it was chronicled by Luke via the Holy Spirit. Upon hearing Apollos speak at the synagogue, they discerned that he was yet ignorant of the full message of Christ despite being a "learned man with a thorough knowledge of the [Old Testament] Scriptures." So they invited him to their home to "explain to him the way of God more adequately," or "more accurately" as some translations put it (verse 26).

Think about it, Priscilla — along with her husband — *taught* this scriptural scholar and mighty speaker New Covenant truths. They did this at their home, which is where most assemblies met back then, in the residences of believers (e.g. Romans 16:3-5 & 1 Corinthians 16:19). In essence, the three of them were "having church." Did not Christ say "where **two or three gather in my name**, there am I with them" (Matthew 18:20)? We have to get away from this idea that believers can only "have church" when they meet at an official Church facility.

Please notice that nothing is said in these passages about how Priscilla, being a woman, should be silent in the church or that she shouldn't teach men, especially someone of Apollos' stature. Nor is anything said about Apollos having a problem receiving from Priscilla. Keep in mind that Apollos was later mentioned in the same breath as Paul and Peter (1 Corinthians 1:12 & 3:22) and Paul placed Apollos on the same spiritual level as himself (1 Corinthians 4:6).

Women who ministered through the Prophetic Word

Philip the evangelist "had four unmarried daughters **who prophesied**" (Acts 21:9). Meanwhile the apostle Paul clearly *expected* women with the prophetic gift to prophesy to others and not keep silent, not to mention pray in public (1 Corinthians 11:4-5); the context implies that men were present. Both passages illustrate the fulfillment of the prophet Joel's word from the LORD: "I will pour out my Spirit on **all people**. Your sons **and daughters** will prophesy" (Joel 2:28 & Acts 2:16-18).

Are these verses referring to the body gift of the prophetic word (Romans 12:6-8) or to the fivefold ministry gift (Ephesians 4:11-13)? If you're unaware, those with the body gift lack the anointing of the fivefold ministry gift. Naturally believers with the body gift, like teaching or prophecy, may eventually be called to serve as fivefold ministers. I'm a good example of this: Before I entered the fivefold ministry I functioned in the Church as a teacher with the body gift. But not all those with a body gift will necessarily go on to serve in the fivefold ministry. It depends on God's will for the believer in question.

Neither passage distinguishes whether these women should use their gift solely in terms of the body gift or also in fivefold ministry, presumably because both apply depending on the individual and her calling. But the main point rings clear: **Women are *expected* to have ministry gifts and serve accordingly.** Read that again; proclaim it from the rooftops.

The female prophet, Anna, is noted when Joseph & Mary brought the child Jesus to the Temple for purification rites. She "spoke about the child **to all** [men and women] who were looking forward to the redemption of Jerusalem" (Luke 2:36-38). While it's debatable whether she was a prophet in the Old Testament sense or the New Testament sense,[2] the fact is that she is chronicled in the

---

[2] See the article *Prophets — New Testament and Old Testament (There's a Difference)* at the Fountain of Life (FOL) site.

New Testament as a prophet and nothing is said about how she should be silent at the Temple and men *shouldn't* listen to her because she's a female. Actually, the passage goes out of its way to point out how devout Anna was and deserving of respect as a godly prophet, not to mention "all" listened to her, not just other women.

Speaking of Mary, she and her relative Elizabeth also served in the prophetic, which we'll look at momentarily.

Additional Women involved in Ministry in the New Testament

Junia

Junia is mentioned along with Andronicus (who may or may not be her husband) as "fellow Jews" who had been in prison with Paul, which shows that they were persecuted for serving the Lord; Paul noted that they were "outstanding among the apostles" and accepted the message of Christ before he did (Romans 16:7). The verse *could* be interpreted to mean that these two were apostles, although the more popular reading is that the apostles held them in high regard due to their devotion to the Lord & ministry.

Phoebe

Phoebe was a deacon (Greek: *diakonos*) at the church in Cenchrea, which means she was involved in helps ministry, assisting the fivefold ministers (Romans 16:1). Deacons today include ushers, greeters, secretaries, custodians and sound operators.

Euodia and Syntyche

These two women "contended at [Paul's] side in the cause of the gospel," which shows that they also functioned in helps ministry as deacons (Philippians 4:2-3).

Lydia

Lydia was a "worshipper of God" from Thyatira that Paul met outside of Philippi. She accepted the message of Christ and invited Paul & his companions to stay at her home with her family (Acts 16:12-15). After Paul & Silas suffered persecution in Philippi they returned to Lydia's house "where they met with the brothers and sisters and encouraged them" (Acts 16:40). Since she actively helped Paul's world-changing ministry she was in essence a deacon.

Lois and Eunice

These women were the grandmother & mother of Timothy respectively; Paul noted their "living faith" that was now living in the young pastor of Ephesus (2 Timothy 1:5). While someone might respond "Whoop-de-do," think about: There is no ministry work more important than raising a child to be an anointed, faithful man or woman of God, especially a powerful fivefold minister, like Timothy, who would reach multitudes (Proverbs 22:6).

Mary, the Mother of Jesus, and Elizabeth

Mary was "highly favored" of the LORD (Luke 1:28) and her relative Elizabeth, a descendent of Aaron, called her "the mother of my Lord" (Luke 1:43). Meanwhile Mary's inspired song revealed that future generations would call her blessed (Luke 1:48). Elizabeth's divine insight and Mary's biblical song places them both **in the prophetic office**.

Mary was also listed with the great leaders of the early Church after the ascension of Christ when the Holy Spirit was about to fall on the believers:

> **Then the apostles returned to Jerusalem from the hill called the Mount of Olives, a Sabbath day's walk from the city. [13]When they arrived, they went upstairs to the room where they were staying. Those present were Peter, John, James and Andrew; Philip and Thomas, Bartholomew and Matthew; James son of Alphaeus and Simon the Zealot, and Judas son of James. [14]They all joined together constantly in prayer, <u>along with the women and Mary the mother of Jesus</u>, and with his brothers.**
>
> **Acts 1:12-14**

Mary, the sister of Martha & Lazarus

This Mary wisely sat at the Lord's feet feeding on his ministry when Jesus visited the siblings' abode (Luke 10:38-42). Christ publicly commended Mary for choosing "what is better" as opposed to Martha who was running around in a distraught whirlwind of preparations. This shows that *relationship* with the Lord takes precedence over *working* for God. Why? Because our work for the Lord should always be a natural outgrowth of our relationship with God. If it's not, we'll fall into the pitfall of legalism, which is counterfeit spirituality.

The Women at Christ's Tomb after his Resurrection

The first persons to discover that the Messiah was resurrected were Mary Magdalene, Mary the mother of James-the-less and Salome (Mark 16:1), but also Joanna & others in the periphery (Luke 24:10). An angel at the tomb told these women to give instructions to Christ's disciples, who would soon be apostles.

As they hurried to fulfill their assignment the resurrected Lord suddenly met them and gave them similar instructions (Matthew 28:1-10 & Mark 16:7). What's the point? **These women were the first evangelists!** Evidently the angel at the tomb and Christ Himself never got the memo that women in the Kingdom of God are to remain silent and *never* instruct a male. Why? Because it's a false doctrine.

Unnamed Women noted in the Book of Acts

Luke spoke of the "prominent women" of Thessalonica and Berea who believed the message of Christ that Paul shared (Acts 17:4 & 17:12). Then there's "the God-fearing women of high standing and the leading men" of Pisidian Antioch (Acts 13:50). While the latter women weren't Christians (yet), Luke spoke of them in noble terms and cited them *before* the leading men of the city. They were open to the gospel of Christ until the legalist Jews stirred up persecution against the ministry of Paul and Barnabas.

The Messiah's attitude toward Women

It's enlightening to observe Jesus' attitude toward women, how he spoke of them and how women were drawn to his benevolent, pure spirit of love:

- Christ took the time to compassionately minister to a Samaritan woman who was an outcast in her community (John 4:4-26). Keep in mind that Hebrews didn't associate with Samaritans because they were a mixed race, the result of the occupation of Israel during the exile, which explains the woman's surprised reaction to Jesus' request in verse 9. Also bear in mind that this woman was five-times divorced and apparently living in fornication with her current mate, which explains why she went to the well alone in the heat of the day.
- The Messiah's profound discussion with the Samaritan woman showed that he respected women and their intelligence; he didn't "dumb things down," which can also be observed in his discussion with Martha about the hope of a resurrection unto eternal life (John 11:17-27).
- While we always hear of the Lord's male disciples, he also had several women who served under his ministry and supported it financially (Luke 8:1-3). They faithfully remained with him in his darkest hour (Matthew 27:55-56).
- Paul also had myriad women serving under his apostleship, some of which were noted earlier in this chapter. Eleven of the 28 people cited in Paul's list in Romans 16 were women, including Phoebe, who delivered his letter.
- Whilst the Lord openly rebuked male religious leaders because they were corrupt, hypocritical and stiff-necked (Matthew 23:13-33 & Luke 11:37-54), he readily forgave

and defended women — and men — who were humbly repentant in response to the Truth (Luke 7:36-50 & John 8:1-11).

- He made sure that some of the illustrations he used in his ministry related to women of that time & place, like a woman making dough (Luke 13:20-21) or sewing a patch of cloth on an old garment (Matthew 9:16-17).

- He included women as the protagonists of his parables, like the one who lost a silver coin and finds it (Luke 15:8-10) and the widow who persistently sought justice from a godless judge (Luke 18:1-8).

- While there are female villainesses in the Bible, such as Jezebel, and the Scriptures warn of the seductress (Proverbs 5:20 & 23:27), no villainess appears in Jesus' parables, although his Parable of the Ten Virgins illustrates that half of the ten were foolish (Matthew 25:1-13).

- The Lord praised the actions of some women, like the one who gave all she had to the Temple treasury (Luke 21:1-4) and the one who anointed him at Bethany in preparation for burial (Mark 14:3-9).

- He commended Mary above Martha for focusing on spending time in his presence and acquiring truth as opposed to blowing time on servile duties (Luke 10:38-42).

- He defended women who suffered abandonment by hardened Israelite husbands that used any excuse to divorce their wives and get someone more desirable (Mark 10:2-12).

- As noted above, women were the initial persons that Christ spoke to after his resurrection and they were the first people he gave an assignment in service of the Kingdom (Matthew 28:1-10 & Mark 16:7). Put another way, the

Lord trusted women to be his first witnesses in a culture that didn't give much recognition to female witnesses.

In none of these examples of women in the New Testament are these ladies spoken of as second-class citizens in the kingdom of God. Nowhere do these verses suggest that women should remain silent at assemblies or that men shouldn't receive from them. Why? Because there is no male or female in Christ (Galatians 3:26-28).

<u>3</u>

Women who Led or Served God in the Old Testament

The Middle East & nearby regions were generally patriarchal in nature, but there are numerous examples of female leaders in the Old Testament, great and small, as well as women who simply served God in one capacity or another. Let's start with…

Deborah

Deborah is one the most notable woman featured in the Old Testament. For twenty years circa 1200 BC, Israel was oppressed by Jabin, king of Canaan. Thus the Lord raised up Deborah:

> Now Deborah, <u>a prophet</u>, the wife of Lappidoth, <u>was leading Israel at that time.</u> [5] She held court under the Palm of Deborah between Ramah and Bethel in the hill country of Ephraim, and <u>the Israelites went up to her to have their disputes</u>

decided. ⁶ She sent for Barak son of Abinoam
from Kedesh in Naphtali and said to him, "The
Lord, the God of Israel, commands you: 'Go,
take with you ten thousand men of Naphtali and
Zebulun and lead them up to Mount Tabor. ⁷ I
will lead Sisera, the commander of Jabin's army,
with his chariots and his troops to the Kishon
River and give him into your hands.' "
⁸ Barak said to her, "If you go with me, I will go;
but if you don't go with me, I won't go."
⁹ "Certainly I will go with you," said Deborah.
"But because of the course you are taking, the
honor will not be yours, for the Lord will deliver
Sisera into the hands of a woman."

Judges 4:4-9

Deborah was married and no doubt submitted to her husband as the
head of the family (Ephesians 5:21-25), but as far as the nation of
Israel was concerned — male and female citizens — she was **1.** a
respected prophet, **2.** a judge who settled legal disputes and **3.** a
military leader. She was such a mighty woman of God that Barak,
a subordinate commander, refused to face the enemy with 10,000
Israelite troops without her presence, even though the LORD
promised to give the Canaanites into Barak's hands (verse 7).

Think about it, **God had no problem with a woman leading the
Israelites *spiritually*, *legally* or *militarily* for 40 years during this
challenging time in Hebraic history.** Female leaders may not
have been the norm since the entire region of the globe was
generally patriarchal, but two chapters of the Holy Scriptures —
God's Word — are devoted to this amazing woman, illustrating
that the Israelites submitted to Deborah spiritually, lawfully and
militarily for four decades!

If this was the way it was when Israel was under the Mosaic Law, a thoroughly inferior covenant, how do you think it is for God's people under the superior New Covenant of grace through Jesus Christ (Hebrews 8:6, 8:13 & 2 Corinthians 3:6)?

One popular minister, who disdains the idea of female leaders — especially spiritual leaders — dismissed the account of Deborah by saying that (paraphrasing) "Deborah's rise to leadership was the exception in the book of Judges because of Barak's failure to show the oomph to lead courageously." Assuming this is so, why didn't the LORD just choose a devout *man* other than Barak to take this supreme position if male leadership is so important and female leadership is unacceptable? I'll tell you why: Because Deborah was the most qualified person for the position and God had zero issue with it. Even the fact that this was largely a patriarchal culture was irrelevant.

Jael

Jael *(yaw-AYL)* was the wife of Heber and is noted in the same chronicling of Deborah and the defeat of the Canaanite forces. The commander of the Canaanites, Sisera, escaped the slaughter of his troops and found refuge in Jael's tent because the Canaanites were on friendly terms with Heber's clan. But Jael was on the side of Israel & Deborah and so brutally drove a tent peg through Sisera's temple into the ground while he slept (Judges 4: 17-21). (She had experience driving tent pegs into the ground and was obviously quite good at it).

Jael is praised in Scripture for her bold actions and called "most blessed of women" (Judges 5:24-27). The very time period was even named after her, as in "the days of Jael" (Judges 5:6).

Needless to say, this is a serious R-rated story and Jael is clearly a mighty warrior-ess of God. I can't help but think of the unnamed woman at Thebez who threw a millstone from the tower, cracking the skull of the fraudulent "king" Abimelech (Judges 9:52-53).

Huldah

Huldah was a respected prophet whom King Josiah contacted via the priests of Jerusalem when the book of the Law was found in the Temple after 55 years of Manasseh's wicked reign. While God pronounced impending judgment upon idolatrous Judah for blatantly forsaking the LORD, righteous Josiah would not see it, but rather live and die in peace (2 Kings 22:14-20).

Noadiah

Noadiah *(no-ad-YAW)* was a prophet in Israel after the exiles returned. She and other seers were evidently in league with Nehemiah's nemesis Sanballat and thus tried to discourage Nehemiah & his team from rebuilding the wall in Jerusalem. Nehemiah prayed that the LORD would help them overcome opposition from such religious leaders (Nehemiah 6:14). It's assumed that God changed the minds of these misguided prophets, particularly after they witnessed the miraculous rebuilding of the walls in 52 days, which resulted in the Great Revival (Nehemiah 8-10). Repentance, by the way, literally means to change one's mind (which naturally results in changed *actions*).

Miriam

This was the sister of Moses and Aaron, who assumed the role of prophet during the exodus from Egypt and led in praise & worship (Exodus 15:20-21).

While her reputation is somewhat soiled by an episode of insubordination and her leprous exile for seven days (Numbers 12 & Deuteronomy 24:9), she was humbled and repented. Is there anyone reading this who hasn't made a huge mistake and repented after being humbled by the LORD? Later prophets of Israel identified Miriam as a leader sent by God, spoken in the same breath as Moses and Aaron (Micah 6:4).

The Queen of Sheba

The queen of Sheba is nameless in the Bible but known as Makeda *(ma-KAY-dah)* in Ethiopian tradition. She came to Jerusalem with a great caravan of gifts for King Solomon wherein she was overwhelmed by Solomon's wisdom and the grandeur of the kingdom of Israel (1 Kings 10:1-13). Another Ethiopian queen is noted a thousand years later in Acts 8:27. In neither case is anything mentioned about how a woman should *not* be a political leader.

Think about it, Solomon was the wisest person on the face of the Earth wherein people from distant lands regularly came to hear his great knowledge, understanding and wisdom (1 Kings 4:29-34). Yet, nowhere does he say anything about it being intrinsically wrong for a woman to lead other people, including men, whether politically, spiritually, judicially or militarily. He doesn't inform the queen of Sheba that she should step down and remain silent in the presence of men. Why not? For one thing, he'd be contradicting God's will when it came to Deborah who led Israel spiritually, legally and militarily a hundred years earlier for forty years.

Abigail

The wise discernment of Abigail saved the lives of all the adult males on her huge ranch after her thankless husband, Nabal *(naw-BAWL)*, showed gross contempt toward the noble David & his warriors. Abigail took the initiative and made the wise decision *without* Nabal's approval to assuage David's righteous anger in order to save the men on her ranch & more (1 Samuel 25). After Nabal's sudden death David sent word to winsome Abigail, asking for her hand in marriage. Obviously "his Momma didn't raise no fool."

Queen Mothers in Israel

'Queen mother' refers to the mother of a reigning monarch who were given the title Gebirah *(gheb-ee-RAW)*, aka "Great Lady," which was an official position in Israel & Judah (1 Kings 15:11-13). Great care was taken to preserve the name of the Queen Mother (e.g. 1 Kings 14:21), although they could be deposed for rebellion against the LORD, as righteous Asa did with his grandmother Maacah (1 Kings 15:13). Nathan the prophet enlisted Bathsheba rather than king David or Solomon in his plan to have Solomon confirmed as king (1 Kings 1:11-40). Wives of kings never ruled Israel or Judah, although the daughters of great allies enjoyed special privileges (1 Kings 7:8) or influence (1 Kings 16:32-33, 18:19 & 21:7-14). However, wicked Queen Mother Athaliah usurped power and became queen of Judah for about seven years after the death of her son by murdering her grandsons, the legitimate heirs. Joash was fortunately able to escape via the aid of Jehosheba (2 Kings 11:1-3).

Unnamed Wise Women during David's Monarchy

A wise woman was specifically sent for by Israel's military commander, Joab, in order to successfully bear a message to the king (2 Samuel 14:1-21).

Later, another wise woman spoke directly to Joab, whose forces were curiously assaulting her righteous city, and she proceeded to advise her fellow citizens on how to end the assault, which they readily heeded (2 Samuel 20:14-22).

Both cases illustrate that these wise women were valued counselors and thus leaders. After all, if people listen to your counsel, you're a leader.

Tamar

God doesn't always spell-out the messages in the various stories in the Bible. There's sometimes an amount of ambiguity that requires reflection and further pursuit for answers. Those who have "ears to hear" will put in the effort while others won't.

Take the fascinating story of Tamar *(taw-MAWR)* and her father-in-law Judah from Genesis 38. Judah unjustly blamed the death of his two sons on Tamar and essentially condemned her to childless widowhood. Tamar understood her father-in-law's fleshly weaknesses and used it to her advantage in a story so sordid it'd be right at home next to any R-rated modern drama. Interestingly, God doesn't spell out the lessons in the story. Judah's hypocrisy is revealed but, at the same time, he should be commended for his honest repentance when confronted with the truth. Tamar's tactics to escape being a childless widow reveal shrewdness and boldness — it guaranteed her security for the future — but does this justify her insidious actions? The Bible doesn't spell-out the answers.

Wisdom is Personified as a Female, Plus the Books of Ruth and Esther

On top of all these examples of notable women in the Bible, I think it's significant to add that wisdom is figuratively personified as a woman in the Old Testament (Proverbs 1:20-33 & Proverbs 8:1-9:12) and two whole books of the Hebraic Scriptures are named *after* mighty women of God, Ruth and Esther. Speaking of those two…

The Book of Ruth depicts the titular woman receiving God's grace and redemption. Tears come to my eyes whenever I read about Moabite Ruth's spirit of faithfulness to her Hebrew mother-in-law, Naomi, who understandably felt forsaken by the LORD in a challenging situation. When Naomi decided to return to Israel from Moab after she caught word of God's provision in the Promised Land, she urged her two widowed daughters-in-law to stay in Moab and find husbands. While one decided to remain, Ruth replied adamantly: "Don't urge me to leave you or to turn back from you. Where you go I will go, and where you stay I will stay. Your people will be my people and your God my God. Where you die I will die, and there I will be buried. May the Lord deal with me, be it ever so severely, if even death separates you and me" (Ruth 1:16-17).

She obviously attracted the LORD's grace because she transferred from poverty to wealth, from widow to wife, from barren to fertile and from foreign outcast to Israelite, not to mention having a place in the lineage of Christ (Matthew 1:1,5)!

The Book of Esther shows the eponymous heroine taking a bold stand to save the Jews who faced great persecution while exiled in Persia. Esther had to do something that was against the law in that kingdom at the penalty of death — appear unsummoned before the Persian king. Nevertheless she promised her godly uncle Mordecai: "I will go to the king, even though it is against the law. And if I perish, I perish" (Esther 4:16).

One unique thing about the book of Esther is that God is never mentioned in any form, although there's evidence of the LORD working behind the scenes, e.g. Ruth 4:14. Why would the Creator allow an entire book in the God-breathed Scriptures that doesn't even mention the LORD? Perhaps God wanted to illustrate that not every expression of ministry has to be overt and that sometimes subtlety is the more effective option.

A good example is this Christian album I bought the other day. A rash critic denounced it on the grounds that "there is no mention of God or Jesus beyond a reference to a 'crown of thorns' in one song." This happened to be the third full-length studio album by this band and there were plenty of references to the Lord in one form or another on their two previous recordings. Obviously the group wanted to take a low-key route for their third effort, which was a concept album. There's nothing wrong with this. Artists have to have the freedom to create as they see fit, presumably led of the Spirit. Without this liberty, we'll fall into a legalistic rut, à la *"Every album must feature a minimum of 7 references to deity; no exceptions!"* (rolling my eyes)

You can look for other notable women in the Old & New Testaments in your studies, such as Rebecca, Leah, Rachel and the other Tamar. I just wanted to establish in these last two chapters several occasions in the Bible where women served God or led others in one capacity or another.

Now let's get back to the Church Age…

4

Can Women Serve as Fivefold Ministers, e.g. Pastors?

We've established that female believers can serve in the Kingdom of God and are expected to, but can they serve in what is known as the fivefold ministry? The fivefold ministry consists of five different offices:

> **So Christ himself gave the <u>apostles</u>, the <u>prophets</u>, the <u>evangelists</u>, the <u>pastors</u> and <u>teachers</u>, [12] to equip his people for works of service, so that the body of Christ may be built up [13] until we all reach unity in the faith and in the knowledge of the Son of God and become mature, attaining to the whole measure of the fullness of Christ.**
> **Ephesians 4:11-13**

When people think of the term 'minister' they automatically think of a pastor, who oversees a local assembly. But this passage plainly shows that professional Christian ministry involves more than pastoring, as important as that service may be.

These five callings in the body of Christ can be summed up briefly as follows:

- **Apostles** like Paul and John have an anointing and drive to go out and start assemblies, as well as oversee them. In order to start or oversee fellowships, an apostle obviously has to have the gift of pastoring. The Scriptures say that a true apostle is marked by "signs, wonders and miracles" (2 Corinthians 12:12), but this might be hard to come by in these days of gross unbelief, although I've seen modern apostles minister in this capacity; they're out there. In any case, apostles should at least have an anointing with the laying on of hands (Hebrews 6:1-2).

- **Prophets** are "interpreters or forth-tellers of the divine will" and should not be confused with that of occultist fortune tellers. The prophetic word is encouraging and is able to touch believers in that specific area where they need ministered, as observed in Acts 15:32. The original Greek word for 'encourage' in this passage means "to cause to move forward." In other words, a prophetic word will inspire believers and spur them to go forward and fulfill God's call on their lives. This shows that prophets are more preachers than teachers. They see things in the spirit realm and proclaim God's will that's applicable to the situation or person, but they don't go into scriptural details on doctrine, like a teacher would.[3]

---

[3] The gift of prophecy in the New Testament era was not given to the body of Christ for the purpose of leading and guiding God's people, as was the case with prophets in the Old Testament, whose prophecies often became Holy Scripture (which explains why their prophecies *had* to be 100% accurate, as observed in Deuteronomy 18:20-22). Why? Because believers are born-again

- **Evangelists** are "bringers of good news," which is what the Greek word means. Like prophets, they're preachers and not teachers. They proclaim by unction the truths of the gospel and the Word of God in general, but they're not effective at detail-oriented teaching. Many hardcore missionaries would be examples of fivefold evangelists. Evangelists can certainly minister to believers at revivals and what have you, but their drive & focus is reaching the lost with the life-changing Good News of the message of Christ (2 Corinthians 5:17-21). Like apostles and prophets, evangelists cited in the New Testament operated in the gifts of the Spirit, such as Philip (Acts 8:4-7, 8:26-40 & 21:8).

- **Pastors** are shepherds in the sense of overseeing a flock of people. Christ of course is the "Good Shepherd" of the worldwide Church (John 10:11,14,27) while pastors are under-shepherds of local assemblies, as observed in 1 Peter 5:1-4. This passage shows that pastors are responsible for **1.** Spiritually feeding the flock of God that is under their care, **2.** "watching over" them, that is, *overseeing* them, **3.** not pursuing dishonest gain, i.e. not being a lover of money, **4.** serving with gratefulness & enthusiasm and not "begrudgingly," **5.** not "lording it over" those entrusted to them but serving with a loving, humble *servant's* heart, and **6.** being examples to "the flock" in all they say and do. This shows that fivefold ministry isn't just about "the ministry of the Word of God" (Acts 6:1-4), but also actually walking

---

spiritually and have the Holy Spirit *within them* for this very purpose. As Jesus said, "But when he, the Spirit of truth, comes, he will guide you into all truth" (John16:13). Since it's the Holy Spirit's job to guide believers in the Church Age, we don't need the gift of prophecy for this function. So when a prophet prophesies over you and says you're to do this or that or go here or there, don't receive it *unless* the Spirit has already been leading you in this direction. In other words, prophecies in the New Testament are to confirm what the Holy Spirit has already been leading you to do. You could say it's an external source to confirm or compliment the believer's internal source of direction from God.

with the Lord and walking in newness of life. In short, it's not just talking the talk, it's walking the walk.

- **Teachers** have the anointing to carefully explain the Holy Scriptures in an understandable, enlightening way. They make the Scriptures come alive for their hearers/readers and help them to see things in God's Word they've never seen before. They give structure to knowledge and their potent insights often result in believers thinking, "I've never heard this, but it makes total sense. Where did s/he get his?!" This is the reaction people had to Christ when he taught (Mark 6:2). It is *teaching* from the Scriptures that feeds people spiritually (Matthew 4:4) whereas *preaching* — the passionate proclaiming of God's Word — motivates people to action. Fivefold teachers differ from pastors (and apostles) in that they don't have the gift to oversee people. I'm a fivefold teacher. I have the gift to teach believers, but not oversee them. To be an effective pastor you have to want to watch over people. I have no such desire. I operate in the ministry of the word (Acts 6:1-4) and pray for my hearers/readers and then it's in the Spirit's hands, as well as the hands of their local pastors.

All fivefold ministers — whether apostles, prophets, evangelists, pastors or teachers — must **1.** walk with God on a daily basis, **2.** know the Holy Scriptures and **3.** be gifted to either teach or preach from them.

The question we want to address is: Can women serve in any of these five positions? We know that Philip the evangelist's four daughters operated in the prophetic (Acts 21:9) and that Priscilla taught Apollos, along with her husband (Acts 18:26), did these women serve with the "body gifts" of prophecy and teaching (Romans 12:6-8) or were they fivefold ministers? I'm assuming the former, but the Bible doesn't distinguish. Furthermore, notice that nowhere in Ephesians 4:11-13 (cited above) does it specify that fivefold ministers *must* be males. Why? Obviously because **"there is no male and female, for you are all one in Christ Jesus"** (Galatians 3:28).

Can Women Serve as Pastors?

An objection to women serving as pastors specifically is based on Paul's instructions to Timothy in Ephesus and Titus in Crete: Paul said that those qualified for the position of pastor must be "faithful to his wife" or "the husband of one wife" (1 Timothy 3:2 & Titus 1:6). Both statements obviously suggest that the pastor is male. But this is easily explained by the fact that these were patriarchal areas and so Paul simply phrased his statements accordingly.

I served under one female pastor for seven years and it sure seemed to me that God was using her in service of the kingdom. This is different than saying that she was a perfect minister; such a person has never existed beyond Jesus Christ (Hebrews 4:15).

For proof that Paul was not excluding the possibility of female pastors in a universal sense throughout the Church Age, he addressed the position of deacons in the very same context with similar instructions: "A deacon must be faithful to his wife and must manage his children and his household well" (1 Timothy 3:12). The Greek word for deacon is *diakonos (dee-AK-on-os)*, which refers to the position of someone in helps ministry, such as an usher, secretary or food distributer. We saw earlier that Phoebe was a deacon at the church in Cenchrea (Romans 16:1) and Euodia & Syntyche were deacons as well (Philippians 4:2-3). As such, Paul's words cannot be interpreted to mean that all deacons must be male during the Church Age. It's an unbiblical position. Since this was the case with deacons, why would it not also be so with pastors?

That said, if you or anyone else is convinced that women should not serve as pastors the answer is simple: Don't go to an assembly with a female pastor; only attend fellowships with male pastors. Problem solved.

As for me & my wife, if the Spirit leads us to serve at an assembly with a female pastor, we're going to follow. People who have qualms about this need not attend.

The Feminine Nature of our Teacher, the Holy Spirit

At this point I think it's important to point out something of which most Christians are not familiar. In the New Covenant **who** is the believer's *spiritual* teacher, that is, their non-human teacher? Answer: **The Holy Spirit is our teacher**, as verified by several verses (John 14:26, Luke 12:12, 1 John 2:20, 2:27 & Nehemiah 9:20). What's interesting is that the Scriptures clearly reveal that the Holy Spirit is *feminine* in nature. Simply consider the evidence…

The creation account of human beings says:

> **So God created man in his own image, in the image of God he created him; male and female he created them.**
>
> **Genesis 1:27**

The word "man" in the Hebrew is *adam*, which is how Adam got his name. However, we see in this text that "man" in the generic sense refers to humankind in general, *both* male and female. And notice that "man" — male *and female* — was created in the image of God. This shows that **the feminine nature originated with the LORD**.

Furthermore, God has a "feminine" side in that Scripture gives evidence of his softer traits (feminine), as well as his sterner side (masculine). Some good examples include Psalm 103:8, 1 John 4:8 and Matthew 11:28-30.

Also consider this verse:

> **<u>As</u> the eyes of slaves look to the hand of their master,**
>   **<u>as</u> the eyes of a female slave look to the hand of her mistress,**
> **<u>so</u> our eyes look to the LORD our God,**
>   **till he shows us his mercy.**
>
>   **Psalm 123:2**

As you can see, the LORD is *compared* with both a master (male) and a mistress (female). And the Creator has no problem including such a passage in the God-breathed Scriptures (2 Timothy 3:16-17). Think about that.

Yet when it comes to Father, Son and Holy Spirit (Matthew 28:19), which one especially suggests the feminine nature? (Please understand that this is not a question of sexuality, but of nature). Obviously not the Father or Son because, after all, they're the **Father** and **Son** — both clearly masculine.

I would offer that the Holy Spirit generally reflects the feminine nature. For instance the symbol for the Holy Spirit is a dove, which suggests beauty, gentleness and harmlessness (Luke 3:22). Also, the Holy Spirit is referred to as a "Helper" of believers in John 14:16,26 (also translated as "Comforter" and "Counselor") and one of Eve's main purposes was to be Adam's "helper" (Genesis 2:18, 20). This same Hebrew word, *ezer (AY-zer)*, is used of God helping believers sixteen times in the Old Testament (e.g. Psalm 115:9-11 & 146:5). In addition, the Holy Spirit is shown to be *sensitive*, easily grieved, in Ephesians 4:30 and Hebrews 10:29, which is more of a feminine characteristic than a masculine one.

Yet the most glaring evidence of the Holy Spirit's feminine nature can be observed in John 3:6 where the Messiah pointed out that "Flesh gives birth to flesh, but **the Spirit gives birth to spirit**." Christ was comparing human birth with spiritual regeneration: Just as a woman gives birth to a child — "flesh gives birth to flesh" — so the Holy Spirit gives rebirth to a person's spirit when s/he turns to God thru Christ. Giving birth clearly bespeaks of the feminine nature. By contrast, in 1 Peter 1:23 believers are said to be "born again" of the imperishable **seed** of the living Word of God, who is Jesus Christ. This is also conveyed in 1 John 3:9 where "seed" in the Greek is *sperma,* the Greek word for sperm. You see, believers are born-again of the sperm of Christ, but **given spiritual rebirth by the Holy Spirit** (Titus 3:5). Giving birth is obviously a feminine quality, not masculine.

Furthermore, this may spur chuckles, but when the Messiah said, "Anyone who speaks a word against the Son of Man will be forgiven, but anyone who speaks against the Holy Spirit will not be forgiven, either in this age or in the age to come" (Matthew 12:32), I can't help but think of the way men get irate when someone says something insulting about their Momma.

In regards to the importance of *not* grieving the Holy Spirit (Ephesians 4:30 & Hebrews 10:29), I can't help but think of the saying: "If Momma ain't happy, no one's happy."

It is true that the Holy Spirit is referred to by the pronoun "he" in Scripture (e.g. John 16:13) and Mary was inseminated by the Holy Spirit (Matthew 1:18-20), but that seed was more specifically the seed of the Word of God, which is Jesus Christ; and the thrust of Scripture points to the Holy Spirit's feminine nature, as detailed above. Besides, God transcends quaint masculine and feminine associations and there is neither male nor female in Christ (Galatians 3:28). Also, Jesus is the wisdom of God, as seen in 1 Corinthians 1:30, but wisdom is personified as a *woman* in Proverbs 8-9 and referred to with a *feminine* pronoun (e.g. Matthew 11:19).

The bottom line is that the believer's spiritual teacher is the Holy Spirit (John 14:26 & 1 John 2:20, 2:27) and the Holy Spirit is clearly feminine in nature. Chew on that.

'But isn't the woman created to be man's helper?'

More specifically, *Eve* was created to be *Adam's* helper because God saw that it wasn't good for Adam to be alone, which happened to be the first thing the LORD said was *not* good in creation (Genesis 2:18). **This shows that men *need* help from women!**

Furthermore, this doesn't mean that women are inferior since — as noted above — the LORD is also described as the helper of God's people in the Old Testament sixteen times using the same Hebrew word, *ezer (AY-zer)*, such as Psalm 124:8. Obviously the LORD is not inferior to human beings; nor is the wife inferior to her husband. This proves, incidentally, that being someone's helper in the sense of *ezer* doesn't mean being a lowly servant girl. After all, is the LORD our lowly servant girl?

So this statement was in reference to *wives* helping *husbands*, but what of the multitudes of women today and throughout history who never marry, as Paul encouraged the female believers of troubled Corinth in 1 Corinthians 7:34? What about women who are widowed or divorced and have no interest in marrying again? Does the fact that they have no husband to assist mean they have no purpose in life? Obviously not. They would use their help-skills to serve the Lord in the Kingdom of God, like Anna did (Luke 2:36-38).

We'll look at how wives are to help husbands & others in greater detail in chapter 7.

'But isn't Man the Head of Woman?'

This question is based on this verse:

> But I want you to realize that the head of every man is Christ, and the head of the woman is man, and the head of Christ is God.
>
> 1 Corinthians 11:3

The koine Greek word for 'woman' is *guné (goo-NAY)*, which is also **the same word used for wife/wives**. In other words, this verse is referring to husbands being the head of the wife, which is stated more specifically in this passage where the Greek for wives/wife is also *guné*:

> ²¹Submit to one another out of reverence for Christ.
> ²²Wives, submit yourselves to your own husbands as you do to the Lord. ²³For the husband is the head of the wife as Christ is the

> **head of the church, his body, of which he is the Savior. [24]Now as the church submits to Christ, so also wives should submit to their husbands in everything.**
> **[25]Husbands, love your wives, just as Christ loved the church and gave himself up for her**
> **Ephesians 5:21-25**

I'm including the bracketing verses because it helps to see the fuller context. Paul starts out by saying that believers are to "submit to one another out of reverence for Christ," which illustrates a spirit of *mutual* submission. We are *all* instructed to make an effort to "get along" and give preference to others in a Christ-like spirit of servanthood. As noted earlier, the Greek word for 'submit' is the same word used for wives submitting to their husbands (Colossians 3:18). This spirit of mutual submission is stressed in other epistles as well; for instance:

- "serve one another humbly in love" (Galatians 5:13),
- "in humility value others above yourselves" (Philippians 2:3), and…
- "All of you, clothe yourselves with humility toward one another, because, 'God opposes the proud but shows favor to the humble'" (1 Peter 5:5).

I'm pointing this out so you clearly see that **submitting to others in a spirit of humility is a universal concept in the body of Christ and not just something wives are to do with their husbands**. Chew on that.

As pointed out in chapter **1**, in the covenant of marriage the husband is the head in the relationship, but this doesn't mean that the two are not equal since 1 Corinthians 11:3 (quoted above) parallels the husband's headship over the wife with God's headship over Christ. Are not the Father and Son equal? Of course they are. Jesus said "I and the Father are one" (John 10:30). Similarly, husbands and wives are ideally supposed to be one (Matthew 19:4-6 & Ephesians 5:31).

Speaking of Ephesians 5, verse 25 instructs husbands to "love your wives, just as Christ loved the Church and gave himself up for her," which shows that **husbands are to love their wives in a self-sacrificial manner**. The Greek word for 'love' in this verse is the verb form of *agapé*, which is defined in the famous love passage 1 Corinthians 13:4-7. It refers to *practical* love and not merely a feeling. If the husband walks in love like this, the wife will gladly submit to his headship. But, again, this does not mean they are not equal nor does it mean the husband is superior. Obviously important issues are discussed at length with much prayer, but someone has to have the final word if the two disagree. After all, when there are two visions there will be di-vision. The idea of headship obviously corresponds to the concept of a chain of command and *not* to the concept of slave and master.

The LORD does not want husbands to lead in an authoritarian sense. This needs stressed because some people automatically equate one person submitting to another with carnal domination. Keep in mind that the devil naturally tries to pervert whatever God creates, commands or blesses. The husband's headship over the wife is paralleled to Father God's headship over Christ (1 Corinthians 11:3), which means it is leadership based on LOVE because "God is love" (1 John 4:7-8,16). This helps make sense of this proverb:

> **Love and faithfulness keep a king safe;**
> **<u>through love</u> his throne is made secure.**
> **Proverbs 20:28**

A "king" refers to an authority figure. In our day and age it would apply to anyone who has authority in any given environment, male or female: a father or mother, a teacher or professor, an employer or supervisor, a president or governor, a pastor or apostle, a police officer or guard, etc. This proverb reveals the *godly* way of keeping one's position of authority — one's "throne" — safe and secure: **Through love and faithfulness**. So, when the Bible talks about leadership and the corresponding submission it's talking about **leading in love and faithfulness**, not being an abusive tyrant. Are you following?

'But isn't Man to "Rule Over" the Woman?'

This question refers to the Genesis curse, which the LORD proclaimed after the fall of Adam & Eve. This was answered in detail in chapter **1**, but to briefly reiterate: The Genesis curse was God's *judgment* on the serpent/satan, Adam & Eve and creation itself, which has negatively affected life on Earth ever since. The Creator's proclamation that the husband would "rule over" the wife in Genesis 3:16 was not a command to Adam, but rather a warning to Eve (and women in general)! It revealed the male's fleshly proclivity to dominate his mate (and women in general) due to normally superior mass & strength, augmented by satan's hatred of women, as noted in verse 15. This was the *result of* sin entering the world, not a command or blessing from God!

Make no mistake the masculine spirit is a *positive* thing and instrumental to a healthy society. The LORD called it "very good" along with everything else that was created (Genesis 1:31). Unfortunately the flesh — the sinful nature — perverts and ruins all good things.

The previous section reveals precisely how God wants males to function as the head in their marriages, which is the furthest thing from being a domineering tyrant. You could say that Ephesians 5:25 and similar verses[4] *counteract* the curse of Genesis 3:16.

As for the erroneous idea that males should "rule over" females in general, if this were so then the LORD wouldn't have chosen Deborah to lead Israel spiritually, judicially and militarily for 40 years in a largely patriarchal region of the globe (Judges 4:4-9).

The fact that males have more muscle mass and are generally more aggressive than females reveals why Peter referred to wives as "the weaker partner," but he said it in the context of instructing husbands to "**be considerate** as you live with your wives, and **treat them with respect** as the weaker partner and **as heirs with you of the gracious gift of life**" (1 Peter 1:7). In other words, God does *not* want husbands treating their wives disrespectfully just because they have more muscles. Wives are just as much heirs of the gracious gift of eternal life as husbands!

'Peter said Wives are to have "a Quiet Spirit"!'

Inspired by the Holy Spirit, Peter encouraged female believers to not focus on "outward adornment" and all that goes with that, but rather on the true attractiveness of "your inner self, the unfading beauty of a gentle and quiet spirit, which is of great worth in God's sight" (1 Peter 1:3-4). He wasn't saying female believers can't wear attractive clothing, just that their focus should be on the true beauty that stems from a spiritual heart. This is what attracted me to Carol, my wife, when I first met her. Of course I found her physically attractive, but she didn't dress like a courtesan and

---

[4] Ephesians 5:28, Colossians 3:19 and 1 Peter 3:7.

didn't need to. It was her gentle, quiet, godly spirit that shown like the midday sun and captured my attention.

By "gentle" and "quiet" I don't mean Carol was a shy pushover, I mean she wasn't an obnoxious loudmouth, like odious LIEberals and their opinionated falsities & slander. There's a pleasantness to a gentle, quiet spirit that doesn't constantly bloviate and isn't rash with jumping to conclusions. At the same time Carol has no qualms about wisely holding me accountable to the Word of God; and I do the same with her, which is a form of tough love. This kind of love doesn't fail to correct others when necessary.

But the Scriptures don't just encourage women to be gentle and quiet as each are positive attributes for *both* men and women. Paul said to all the believers at Philippi: "Let your gentleness be evident to all" (Philippians 4:5). Meanwhile James said "**Everyone** should be quick to listen, slow to speak and slow to become angry" (James 1:19). And the book of Proverbs says "The one who has knowledge <u>uses words with restraint</u>, and whoever has understanding is <u>even-tempered</u>" (Proverbs 17:27).

In other words, the Scriptures exhort *both* men and women to **not** be loathsome loudmouths. Yet this doesn't mean there isn't a time & place for righteous reprimand and Holy Ghost-inspired preaching.

5

1 Corinthians 14:34-35

This brings us to two statements by Paul in the New Testament that *seem* to contradict everything we've been seeing in the Scriptures up to this point about women in God's service. However, the Bible is "God-breathed" (2 Timothy 3:16-17) and does not contradict itself when properly understood through the use of common sense hermeneutical guidelines, like "Scripture interprets Scripture" and "Context is King."

So let's examine both texts and consider reasonable interpretations that gel with the context of the passage and what the rest of Scripture says about women in the LORD's service.

Establishing Order in the Assemblies so that the Believers would be Edified

The topic in the latter section of 1 Corinthians 14 is effective ministry and maintaining order when the troubled church in Corinth assembled. This is important to know because "Context is King" and thus understanding the context will naturally help us to properly interpret the passage in question. Here's how the section opens:

> **What then shall we say, brothers and sisters? When you come together, each of you has a hymn, or a word of instruction, a revelation, a tongue or an interpretation. <u>Everything must be done so that the church may be built up</u>.**
>
> **1 Corinthians 14:26**

First, notice that Paul is addressing both males *and* females in the assembly, which can also be verified by Paul's greeting at the beginning of this letter:

> **<u>To the church of God in Corinth</u>, <u>to those sanctified in Christ Jesus</u> and called to be <u>his holy people</u>, together with <u>all those everywhere who call on the name of our Lord Jesus Christ</u>— their Lord and ours:**
>
> **1 Corinthians 1:2**

The Greek word for "brothers and sisters" in verse 26 is *adelphos (ad-el-FOS)*, which is a masculine noun, but is gender neutral in usage, similar to the English 'guys.' I've done sermons where I've addressed the congregants as "guys," but I was obviously referring to both males and females. That's the case here. For scriptural proof, look no further than Romans 16:1-17 where Paul is clearly addressing males *and* females in the Church and then refers to them collectively as *adelphos* in verse 17. This explains why some translations, such as the NIV and NASB, translate *adelphos* as "brothers and sisters" here and not just "brothers." It's simply more accurate since Paul was addressing both men and women.

Now notice that Paul says, "When you come together, <u>each of you</u> has a hymn, or a word of instruction, a revelation, a tongue or an interpretation. Everything must be done so that the church may be built up" (verse 26). The Greek word for "each of you" is *hekastos (HEK-as-tos)*, which comprises *both* genders, not just males. Each of the believers would have something to give when they gathered together, male and female, but Paul was concerned about maintaining a sense of order. Paul's goal was that **the church be built up when assembled**. "The church" refers to the people, not the building where they happened to meet. So the goal was for *believers* to be **built-up**.

Three Sets of People at the Corinthian Church were instructed to Keep Quiet

Paul then proceeds to give instructions on public tongues & interpretation, as well as prophecies. If you've never been to a Christian assembly that believes in charismatic gifts you might be unfamiliar with them, but 1st Century fellowships regularly flowed in these gifts as evident in Paul's letter. It's a shame that the false doctrine of cessationism and the corresponding unbelief have all but eliminated these wonderful gifts from our assemblies.[5]

---

[5] Cessationism *(seh-SAY-shun-izm)* is the erroneous belief that gifts of the Spirit (1 Corinthians 12:4-11) ceased by the end of the 1st Century when the last of the original apostles passed away and the biblical canon was completed. While most adherents of cessationism believe God still performs miracles, they don't believe that the LORD works miracles through the gifts of the Spirit any longer. Nor do they believe that the ministerial offices of the apostle and prophet — with the signs & wonders thereof — are in operation today; they believe these ceased when what they call the 'Apostolic Age' ended. Cessationists suggest that 1 Corinthians 13:8-12 supports this theory but this text obviously contrasts our life on this Earth where "we see in a mirror dimly" with life on the other side of glory being "face to face" with our Creator; *now* we only "know in part" whereas *then* we shall "know fully" even as we are now "fully known" by the LORD (verse 12). The glaring problem with the religious doctrine of

A Side Note: The gift of public tongues is not the same as private glossolalia, which is synonymous with praying in the spirit. The former is a gift of the Spirit (1 Corinthians 12:4-11) wherein God speaks to people thru the gift of tongues manifesting in a believer as the Spirit wills whereas praying in the spirit is the believer using the gift of glossolalia to pray to God by the Spirit (1 Corinthians 14:14-15). One is *God speaking to believers* while the other is *the believer praying to God* bypassing the limitations of his/her mind.[6]

Paul defends order for the mutual good of all the believers present. He naturally wants those with spiritual gifts and those who disrupt the service to respect others present. Here are the three sets of people he instructs to keep quiet:

1. Those openly speaking in tongues who didn't have an interpretation or interpreter (verse 28). These people were basically pretending like they had the gift of the Spirit of public tongues, but they didn't, which explains why there was no interpretation. Hence Paul instructs them to keep quiet and speak in tongues to God privately without disturbing the congregation.
2. Those ministering in prophecy when the Spirit moves upon someone else to prophesy (verse 30). Such believers were obviously hogging the stage, so to speak. These kinds of people are basically arrogant loudmouths — the opposite of humility — and God *opposes* arrogance (James 4:6).
3. Wives who were blurting out during the service and thus disrupting the ministry (verse 34).

---

cessationism is that it encourages believers to *deny* what the New Testament Scriptures plainly instruct us to eagerly desire: Believers are exhorted to **"eagerly desire"** spiritual gifts (1 Corinthians 12:1,31 & 14:1,39) while cessationism encourages believers to do **the precise opposite**.

[6] For details see the article *Baptism of the Holy Spirit — and It's Benefits* at the FOL site.

The Greek word for keeping quiet in all three verses is *sigaó (see-GAH-oh)*, which means to keep silent or keep a secret. In short, all three sets of people were to keep unedifying things to themselves during the service. Yet none of these three prohibitions against speaking was absolute:

1. Those speaking in tongues should only keep quiet if they didn't have the gift of the Spirit to edify the congregation, but this didn't mean they wouldn't use their gift of glossolalia to pray to God privately by the Spirit, as Paul himself did (1 Corinthians 14:13-19).
2. Those prophesying should only keep silent when the Spirit gives a prophetic word to another believer, but this didn't mean they should never prophesy in the assembly.
3. Just the same, wives who were disrupting the service by blurting out questions and other things should keep quiet at this time, but this didn't mean they should *never* speak at the assembly.

The apostle points out: "For God is not a God of disorder but of peace — as in all the congregations of the Lord's people" (verse 33). So, again, Paul was concerned about establishing a sense of order in the assemblies at Corinth and eliminating selfishness so that believers would leave the meeting built up and not unedified & frustrated. Obviously the Corinthian fellowships had an issue with disorder when they met, which is plainly indicated in earlier verses of the epistle (1 Corinthians 1:10-17 & 3:1-5).

The Passage in Question

This is when Paul says:

64

Women should remain silent in the churches. They are not allowed to speak, but must be in submission, as the law says. ³⁵If they want to inquire about something, they should ask their own husbands at home; for it is disgraceful for a woman to speak in the church.

³⁶Or did the word of God originate with you? Or are you the only people it has reached? ³⁷If anyone thinks they are a prophet or otherwise gifted by the Spirit, let them acknowledge that what I am writing to you is the Lord's command. ³⁸But if anyone ignores this, they will themselves be ignored.

1 Corinthians 14:34-38

Again, Paul didn't mean that women should remain silent in assemblies in an absolute sense. After all, he stated earlier that women with the prophetic gift are expected to prophesy to others and not keep silent, not to mention pray in public (1 Corinthians 11:4-5). Furthermore, as noted above, he said that each of them — male and female — would have a hymn, or a word of instruction, a revelation, a tongue or an interpretation when they assembled, which naturally involves speaking during the assembly (verse 26).

"Wives [who Disrupt the Services] should remain Silent during the Church Service"

Secondly, the phrase "Women should remain silent in the churches" would more accurately be translated as "wives should remain silent when the church assembles" for these two reasons:

1. The koine Greek word for "women" is *guné (goo-NAY)*, which is also **the same word used for wife/wives**, as observed in verses like Matthew 1:20,24.
2. Paul follows up this statement with "If they want to inquire about something, **they should ask their *own husbands* at home**." Since not every single woman had a husband, verse 34 *must* be referring to wives.

Keep in mind that the topic was keeping a sense of order when the believers gathered for a service, which is why Paul concludes with "be eager to prophesy, and do not forbid speaking in tongues. But everything should be done in a fitting and orderly way" (verses 39-40). Apparently wives were blurting out questions and perhaps other things during the service, which wasn't helped by the possibility that women and men were seated in different areas. This inclination may have been due to their newfound sense of freedom in Christ or the negative influence of Dionysian worship and Gnosticism in the area (which we'll look at shortly). Whatever the case, their selfish outbursts naturally created an atmosphere of disorder and Paul wanted to put a stop to it.

A good modern example would be this woman at one assembly where I frequently taught years ago. She would occasionally blurt out questions during the sermon, which disrupted the ministry of the word. One day my wife happened to be sitting behind her at a service when she uttered a question; Carol tapped her shoulder and kindly whispered "Jessie, why don't you save your questions till after the service, Dirk's trying to minister the word and it's being recorded." Of course Carol didn't *want* to say this since it could be misconstrued as unkind, but the situation called for it and it effectively restored order. I'm sure Paul didn't want to include verses 34-35 in his letter, but the situation demanded it.

Being Sensitive to the Customs of the Culture in order to Effectively Minister there

About ten years after Paul wrote this letter to the Corinthian believers he wrote to Titus who was pastoring on the island of Crete:

> **Likewise, teach <u>the older women</u> to be reverent in the way they live, not to be slanderers or addicted to much wine, but to <u>teach what is good</u>. ⁴Then they can urge the younger women to love their husbands and children, ⁵to be self-controlled and pure, to be busy at home, to be kind, and <u>to be subject to their husbands, so that no one will malign the word of God</u>.**
>
> **Titus 2:3-5**

Seasoned, reverent Christian women on Crete were instructed and expected to "teach what is good." While this likely refers to the body gift of teaching (Romans 12:6-8) and not the fivefold ministry gift (Ephesians 4:11-13), it's not technically distinguished. Paul adds that these women should be subject to their husbands at home "so that no one will malign the word of God." This shows that Paul was sensitive to the positive image of Christianity in a rigidly patriarchal culture obviously so that the spread of the word of God would not be hindered.

To explain, while Paul plainly declared by the Spirit in one of his earliest epistles that "there is no male and female, for you are all one in Christ Jesus" (Galatians 3:28), he was also conscious of the male-dominated cultures of which Titus and other pastors ministered and he didn't want the word of God to be "maligned" — written off — because it alienated citizens since it didn't align with the ethos of their societies. The Greek word ethos *(EE-thaws)* originally meant "accustomed place" and refers to customs of a particular culture, equivalent to the Latin word mores.

The Middle Eastern custom of men being the rulers of their households can be observed in the king of Persia's edict after Queen Vashti disobeyed him (Esther 1:20-22). This was not Old Testament law, but rather a *Persian* edict. It illustrates the general patriarchal air of the region.

A good parallel in the modern world would be a Christian ministry trying to pioneer assemblies in a strict Muslim nation once the government finally permits an openly Christian fellowship. For such a mission to succeed they'd have to work *within* the cultural framework of that region; they'd have to be considerate of that area's established mores. As such, they obviously wouldn't send a woman to pastor an assembly nor female evangelists to conduct services, like Amie Semple McPherson or Kathryn Kulman. The patriarchal culture of Tehran observed in the book & movie *Not Without My Daughter* is a good example (which was corroborated in the daughter's account, *My Name is Mahtob*).

Think about it in terms of the USA, a generally liberal "first world" country (which is where I live): Women didn't even get the right to vote until 1920. Since then ladies have made much progress in walking free of the curse of Genesis 3:16 but, before that, we were very much a patriarchal society and women in ministry were few and far between. Even today female ministers are by far the minority and they *still* catch flak for openly serving in God's kingdom, especially if they function as pastors.

Since the USA and Western nations in general — including Western-influenced countries — are no longer rigidly patriarchal there's no reason women cannot serve in the fivefold ministry when called. Of course, ministers have to be led of the Spirit to serve effectively in whatever pocket of the country they're assigned. For instance, there's a vast difference between serving in Los Angeles and ministering in a hamlet of the Deep South.

Paul's sensitivity to cultural mores so as not to "hinder the gospel" can be observed earlier in his epistle to the Corinthians when he discussed the wearing of hats during prayer and men's hair length (1 Corinthians 11:2-16). Neither of these had anything to do with Christian morality, but rather respect for the customs of the culture in question so as not to impede the spread of the message of Christ. Just the same, he was sensitive to the patriarchal nature of the areas where some of his subordinates ministered. It's the principle of "becoming all things to all people so that by all possible means [we] might save some," which Paul stressed earlier in his letter (1 Corinthians 9:19-23).

In America today there's cultural diversity and therefore respect or tolerance for different styles & customs of a culture or subculture. Despite this, a friend of mine who's a fulltime evangelist informed me that "older viewers" might be turned off by the "head piece" I wore in my video *Four Rules of Bible Interpretation*, which is on Youtube. I didn't take him in the wrong spirit because he was just concerned about reaching as many people as possible and not unnecessarily turning some off. Paul had a similar concern in the mid-1st Century with the assemblies he oversaw in regards to the customs of the area in question. Nevertheless, I didn't change the video because it reflects America's modern subcultural diversity. If anyone is offended by what I wear on my head they don't have to watch it.

Bacchus/Dionysus Worship in Corinth

The situation in 1st Century Corinth may be better grasped when you understand that the female-dominated worship of Bacchus was prevalent. Bacchus is better known as Dionysus, the Greco-Roman deity of the grape harvest & winemaking, as well as fertility, ritual madness and religious ecstasy. Ancient writers described Dionysian celebrants as engaging in excessive behavior, like drunkenness, revelry, sexual promiscuity and degrees of undress. It was all about the instinctual, the spontaneous and the emotional at the expense of moderation. Is it any wonder that Jim Morrison of The Doors was heavily into Dionysus? Imagine the activity at one of that group's more wild concerts in the late 60s and that's in essence Dionysian worship.

Female devotees of Bacchus/Dionysus were called maenads *(MAY-nids)*, literally "mad women" or "raving ones." When they worked themselves into a frenzy during their pagan gatherings they would cry out or offer a high pitched chant accompanied by clanging cymbals. They were occasionally known to tear animals limb from limb, consuming them bloody raw as part of their perverted worship. There are even legends of them tearing men limb from limb, e.g. Pentheus and Orpheus. Is it any wonder that Alexander the Great reportedly incorporated these fierce maenads into his army to assist in conquering lands?

Just as new believers today tend to retain elements of their subcultures (e.g. punks, rappers and Goths), so ex-worshipers of Dionysus at the assemblies in Corinth no doubt retained a residue of their former lifestyles, particularly the more recent female converts. This is hinted at in several of Paul's statements in his letter:

- Believers with weak consciences being uncomfortable with the idea of other believers eating meat sacrificed to idols (1 Corinthians 8:1-13).
- Paul's condemnation of partaking of sacrificial meals in pagan temples (1 Corinthians 10: 14-22).
- Believers getting drunk during Holy Communion (1 Corinthians 11:21). Talk about disorder!
- Paul's critical reference to the noise of a resounding gong or clanging cymbal (1 Corinthians 13:1).

The point is that women in Corinth were negatively swayed by the Dionysian culture of their area and this understandably affected order in the relatively new Christian services. Paul was just trying to get the pandemonium under control.

The Proper Reading of 1 Corinthians 14:34-35

Based on what we now know from the above facts, let's reread the text in question juxtaposed with a paraphrased rendition:

> **Women should remain silent in the churches. They are not allowed to speak, but must be in submission, as the law says. [35]If they want to inquire about something, they should ask their own husbands at home; for it is disgraceful for a woman to speak in the church.**
>
> **1 Corinthians 14:34-35**

> **Wives** [who blurt out things] **should remain silent when the church assembles. They are not allowed to speak, but must be in submission** [to their husbands]**, as the law says. [35]If they want to inquire about something, they should ask their**

own husbands at home; for it is disgraceful for a [selfish, disrupting] **wife to blurt out things during the service.**

1 Corinthians 14:34-35 (paraphrased)

This is the proper reading of the passage since it doesn't contradict the rest of Scripture.

'What about the Statement They "Must be in Submission, <u>as the Law Says</u>"?'

Paul's issue was wives blurting out questions and other things during the service at the Corinth assemblies, which interrupted the ministry of the word. This is why he followed up with "If they want to inquire about something, they should ask their own *husbands* at home." So, as far as submission goes, Paul was specifically talking about wives being submissive to their husbands. In chapters <u>1</u> and <u>4</u> we saw that Paul actually taught *all* believers are to be submitted to one another with a humble, servant's heart, which he stated *before* he instructed wives to submit to their husbands (Ephesians 5:21-25). So the attitude of submission is a universal dynamic in the body of Christ and not just something for wives to do with their husbands.

Furthermore, Paul paralleled the husband's headship over the wife to Christ's headship over the Church. Does the Lord lead believers in a carnally controlling way? Of course not. Yeshua leads by laying down his life for his beloved. Husbands are instructed to lead **in the same manner**, not "rule over" their wives in a fleshly tyrannical way. When Paul elsewhere instructed wives to submit to their husbands "as is fitting in the Lord" he immediately followed it up with "Husbands, **love your wives** and **do not be harsh with**

them" (Colossians 3:18-19). So the idea of men "ruling over" their wives in a carnal way is completely out of the picture.

As for Paul's statement that wives must be in submission "as the Law says," this was not a reference to the curse of Genesis 3:16 since that was *a curse* — a punishment for disobedience — not a moral command (law) or blessing. Actually it was a *warning* to Eve, and women in general, of how carnally-controlled men would try to dominate them since they have more brawn and aggression, generally speaking. Because there is no *specific* statement in the Old Testament Scriptures about wives submitting to their husbands, Paul must have been referring to the *gist* of the Law, as observed in Numbers 30 and Genesis 2:18.

Keep in mind, however, that there are several passages in the Old Testament that reveal how valuable a noble wife is — and women in general — such as:

> **A wife of noble character is her husband's crown,**
> **but a disgraceful wife is like decay in his bones.**
> **Proverbs 12:4**

> **The wise woman builds her house,**
> **but with her own hands the foolish one tears hers down.**
> **Proverbs 14:1**

> **He who finds a wife finds what is good**
> **and receives favor from the LORD.**
> **Proverbs 18:22**

¹⁰ A wife of noble character who can find?
    She is worth far more than rubies.
¹¹ Her husband has full confidence in her
    and lacks nothing of value.
¹² She brings him good, not harm,
    all the days of her life.
¹³ She selects wool and flax and works with eager hands.
¹⁴ She is like the merchant ships, bringing her food from afar.
¹⁵ She gets up while it is still night;
    she provides food for her family
    and portions for her female servants.
¹⁶She considers a field and buys it;
    out of her earnings she plants a vineyard.

                    Proverbs 31:10-16

²⁵She is clothed with strength and dignity;
    she can laugh at the days to come.
²⁶She speaks with wisdom,
    and faithful instruction is on her tongue.

                    Proverbs 31:25-26

Wow, this just abolishes the whole "The Old Testament is misogynistic" theory, doesn't it?

We'll look at further insights along these lines in chapter **7**.

<u>6</u>

1 Timothy 2:11-15

Let's now look at the other seeming "hard saying" concerning women in the New Testament:

> **A woman should learn in quietness and full submission. [12]I do not permit a woman to teach or to assume authority over a man; she must be quiet. [13]For Adam was formed first, then Eve. [14]And Adam was not the one deceived; it was the woman who was deceived and became a sinner. [15]But women will be saved through childbearing — if they continue in faith, love and holiness with propriety.**
>
> **1 Timothy 2:11-15**

Here Paul is writing his protégé Timothy who was pastoring in Ephesus, located in what is today western Turkey. When he says that "women should learn in quietness and full submission" he was obviously referring to *wives* submitting to *their* husbands since he goes on to reference the first husband & wife of humanity, Adam and Eve. Remember, as noted in the previous two chapters, the koine Greek word for "women," *guné (goo-NAY)*, can refer to either women or wives depending on the context. For instance, in Matthew 19:9 it clearly refers to a wife.

This is further reinforced by the fact that Paul taught elsewhere in the New Testament that wives were to submit to their husbands (Ephesians 5:21-25 & Colossians 3:18-19), as did Peter (1 Peter 3:1), *because* the husband has headship in the marriage, which is likened to Father God's headship in relation to the Son (1 Corinthians 11:3 & 15:27-28). This has to do with the chain of authority in the family and does not indicate inequality or superiority as the Scriptures clearly state that God is one and thus Father & Son are one (Deuteronomy 6:4, John 10:30 & John 1:1-4). Ideally, husbands & wives are to be one as well with the wife submitting to the husband just as the Son submits to the Father.

So when Paul says "I do not permit a woman to teach or to assume authority over a man; she must be quiet" he was referring to wives submitting to their husbands as the head in the marriage. Obviously there was an issue with wives disrespecting their husbands in the Ephesian assemblies or disrupting the services in some way, similar to the situation ten years earlier in Corinth. The Greek word for "assume authority" is *authenteó (aw-then-TEH-oh)*, which is used this sole time in Scripture. In the Greek literature of that era the term had a radical connotation as in exercising authority in a domineering manner, even resorting to murder. Paul was led of the Spirit to use this more extreme term for exercising authority above a more common one, which points to the nature of the problem in Ephesus.

In regards to cultural context, pertinent background info reveals the zeitgeist of that area, which had an impact on the believers at Ephesus...

The Cult of Artemis at Ephesus and the Philosophy/Religion of Gnosticism

The worship of the goddess Artemis *(ART-uh-mis)* was big in Ephesus where its Temple of Artemis was one of the Seven Wonders of the Ancient World. Paul spent three and a half years establishing the church in Ephesus and, at one point, caused a riot because the message of Christ was turning so many people away from the idolatry of Artemis, which resulted in craftsmen losing business making idols (Acts 19: 23-41).

Artemis worship was a female-dominated cult that believed Artemis was born before her male twin Apollo and thus women were superior to men and could dominate them. So Paul was countering this belief with his instructions in 1 Timothy 2:11-15 and this explains his point that "Adam was formed first, then Eve."

Paul went on to stress that "Adam was not the one deceived; it was the woman who was deceived and became a sinner." In other words, Eve was the first to sin, *then* Adam, which would taint the human race yet in their loins. Again, Paul was counteracting false beliefs promoted by the Artemis cult. But there's something obvious that needs added to his commentary for balance: Eve was deceived into sinning whereas Adam sinned *without* being deceived, likely because feminine beauty was his weakness and so he just went along with Eve's transgression.

The apostle was simultaneously counteracting the false religion/philosophy of Gnosticism *(NOSS-tuh-sism)* prevalent in the region, which taught that the woman was the originator of man and that the serpent in the Eden story was good — merely trying to get Eve to eat of the Tree of Gnosis *(NOH-sis)*, aka the Tree of Knowledge, in an effort to *enlighten* Adam.

So Paul was "killing two birds with one stone" with his instructions in 1 Timothy 2:11-14.

What does "Women will be Saved through Childbearing" Mean?

This brings us to Paul's curious statement in verse 15:

> **But women will be saved through childbearing—**
> **if they continue in faith, love and holiness with**
> **propriety.**
>
> **1 Timothy 2:15**

More literally, women will be saved through *the* childbearing, a reference to the incarnation of Christ — the birth of Jesus into this world. Recall what the LORD prophesied over satan during the Genesis curse:

> **And I will put enmity**
> **between you [satan] and the woman,**
> **and between your offspring and hers [Christ];**
> **he [Christ] will crush your head,**
> **and you will strike his heel."**
>
> **Genesis 3:15**

The mighty Messiah crushed satan's head through his birth, death and resurrection. As it is written: "The reason the Son of God appeared was **to destroy the devil's work**" (1 John 3:8).

This is the obvious interpretation of the verse since the idea that women are saved through merely bearing children doesn't even make sense. The Scriptures plainly teach that we are saved by God's graciousness through faith in Christ, not by works, although genuine faith always results in works (Ephesians 2:8-9 & James 2:14-26).

Paul's additional statement that women will be saved through *the* childbearing of Christ *"if* they continue in faith, love and holiness with propriety" merely points to the necessity of *persevering* in faith, which he stressed elsewhere to *all* believers, not just women (Colossians 1:22-23). After all, if it takes faith to be saved it naturally follows that someone *cannot* be saved if they come to a point where they no longer believe due to neglecting the feeding of their faith.[7]

How Do We Know that Paul *wasn't* saying All Women should Submit to All Men?

Some people have gone to extremes with Paul's statement: "A woman should learn in quietness and full submission. I do not permit a woman to teach or to assume authority over a man; she must be quiet" (1 Timothy 2:11-12), suggesting that women should submit to men in general. But such a radical interpretation can be dismissed for a dozen glaring reasons:

- As already covered, Paul was talking about wives submitting to husbands as the head in the marriage in the same manner that the Son submits to the Father as head.
- Suggesting that all women should submit to all men in general would contradict the LORD's choosing of Deborah to lead Israel for 40 years spiritually, legally and militarily (Judges 4:4-9).

---

[7] For details see the article *Once Saved Always Saved?* at the FOL site.

- It would contradict God's usage of several notable women in the Old Testament who taught males, like the prophet Huldah (2 Kings 22:14-20).
- It would contradict the instructions of the angel at Christ's tomb and the Messiah Himself that were given to several women who visited the empty tomb. They were instructed to educate men — Jesus' imminent apostles — and thus these women became the first evangelists (Mark 16:1, Luke 24:10, Matthew 28:1-10 & Mark 16:7).
- It would contradict Priscilla's teaching of the mighty scholar Apollos "more accurately" at her home along with her husband (Acts 18:24-26). By the way, a portion of the church in Ephesus — the town in which Timothy ministered — met in Priscilla & Aquila's abode there (1 Corinthians 16:19).
- It would contradict Paul's commendation of Timothy's grandmother & mother — Lois and Eunice — for being responsible for Timothy's "living faith" (2 Timothy 1:5 & Proverbs 22:6).
- Moreover, Timothy traveled & ministered with Paul as his protégé in the past (1 Corinthians 4:17). If Paul had a universal rule against women teaching men Timothy would've already known about it.
- In 1 Corinthians 14:26 Paul addresses believers with the Greek word *adelphos (ad-el-FOS)*, which refers to males *and* females in practice, similar to how we use the English 'guys.' This is verified by his usage of the word in Romans 16:17 where he was clearly referring to men *and* women. Moreover Paul goes on to say "When you come together, each of you has a hymn, or a word of instruction, a revelation, a tongue or an interpretation"; the Greek word for "each of you" is *hekastos (HEK-as-tos)*, which is gender neutral and can refer to males and/or females. In other words, when believers come together women, as well

as men, can have a word of instruction — a teaching — and are expected to voice it.

- Paul lists the body gifts that are available to all believers in 1 Corinthians 12:4-11, which includes the gift of teaching. In Ephesians 4:11-13 he lists the fivefold ministry gifts, which also includes the gift of teaching. Nowhere in either context does Paul stipulate that only males can have these gifts and use them. Why not? Obviously because they're available to men and women and *both* are expected to walk in them.

- Paul admonished the believers in Colosse to "teach and admonish one another with all wisdom through psalms, hymns, and songs from the Spirit" (Colossians 3:16). The opening of that epistle shows that Paul was writing the "saints" in Colosse and referred to them with the aforementioned Greek word *hekastos* (Colossians 1:2) which, again, refers to males *and* females, as proven by Romans 16:17. Once more, he doesn't stipulate that only males should be teaching and admonishing others.

- In his second letter to Timothy, Paul instructs his protégé to "entrust to reliable people" what he has taught him "who will also be qualified to teach others" (2 Timothy 2:2). The word 'people' is *anthrópos (ANTH-ro-pos)*, which refers to human beings in general, not just males. It's where we get the English word anthropology.

- Christ rebukes the believers at Thyatira for tolerating the teachings of "Jezebel" in Revelation 2:20-23. Nowhere does the Lord suggest that it's wrong for a woman to teach; the issue was *what* this particular woman taught, which misled Christians into sexual immorality and idolatry. It's actually implied that it's perfectly appropriate for a woman to teach and other believers would listen, including males.

The Proper Understanding of 1 Timothy 2:11-15

So Paul was talking about wives submitting to their husbands in 1 Timothy 2:11-15, not all women submitting to every man on Earth, which would be absurd, then or now. The passage should be read thusly:

> **A wife should learn in quietness and full submission.** [12] **I do not permit a wife to teach or to** [radically] **assume authority over her husband; she must be quiet** [and respect her husband in the assembly]. [13] **For Adam was formed first, then Eve.** [14] **And Adam was not the one deceived; it was his wife who was deceived and became a sinner.** [15]**But she will be saved through the childbearing** [i.e. Christ's incarnation, death and resurrection] — **if she continues in faith, love and holiness with propriety.**
>
> 1 Timothy 2:11-15 (paraphrased)

Paul was led of the Spirit to stress this because there was a spirit of misandry in Ephesus due to the influence of Artemis worship and Gnosticism. This was manifesting in marriages in the Ephesian church and it was a glaring enough issue that word traveled to Paul about it, whether through Timothy or others.

For anyone who doesn't know, misandry *(mis-ANN-dree)* is the opposite of misogyny. The latter is the devaluing, disrespect or abuse of women while the former is contempt for men. There's a growing spirit of misandry in the USA today and Western nations in general, which can be observed in the popular phrase "toxic masculinity" and the emergence of 'soy boys.' I'm not saying there isn't such a thing as negative masculinity. Obviously there is, but let's not mistakenly turn to misandry to purge it. Let's also not cultivate a spirit of toxic femininity, which is just as damaging as toxic masculinity.

Speaking of toxic femininity and the corresponding misandry, this was obviously a serious enough problem in Ephesus due to Artemis worship and Gnosticism for Paul to address it so overtly.

Properly Understanding the Husband's Headship in the Marriage

Just as there cannot be a healthy marriage if a spirit of misogyny is prevalent, the same is true if there's a spirit of misandry. The Holy Spirit, working through Paul, wanted to ensure that there were *healthy* marriages in the assemblies in Ephesus.

We've already gone over the fact that a husband being the head in the family does not mean there's inequality between the husband and wife since the Father is head of the Son and yet they are equal (1 Corinthians 11:3, Genesis 1:26, John 10:30 & 1 Corinthians 3:23). In other words, headship does *not* mean better. God gave *both* Adam & Eve the commission to subdue or govern the Earth, not just Adam (Genesis 1:28). Nor is headship an excuse for abuse since husbands are plainly exhorted to *love* their wives in the self-sacrificial sense of Christ loving the Church; and they are *not* to be harsh with them (Ephesians 5:25 & Colossians 3:19).

Another thing that needs to be understood is that the husband is the head of the marriage & family in the sense of the chain of authority, **but**...

1. The wife is the *domestic* head as observed later in Paul's letter to Timothy where he instructed younger widows "to manage their homes" (1 Timothy 5:14). This phrase is one compound word in the Greek, *oikodespoteó (oy-kod-es-pot-EH-oh)* meaning "to rule the household." This explains why our great father of faith, Abraham, complied with Sarah's important domestic decisions (e.g. Genesis 21).[8]

2. The husband is not the spiritual head because Christ is the spiritual head since he's the head of the worldwide Church, the body of Christ (Ephesians 1:22, 4:15, 5:23 & Colossians 1:18); thus the Lord is the spiritual head of every female believer, including wives. If this were not the case it would mean that an unbelieving husband would be the spiritual head of a believing wife, which is obviously not the case (1 Corinthians 7:13-16). That said, a husband *can* be the subordinate spiritual head of the marriage & family — subordinate to Christ, of course — *if* he proves himself faithful and devoted to the Lord.

I say "if" because some Christian husbands don't prove themselves worthy of subordinate spiritual headship in the marriage. For instance, I know a couple who used to attend an assembly I taught at in the 2000s where the husband would often lead in worship, playing piano and singing. He was a gifted worship leader, but in

---

[8] This also explains an interpretation of a statement in 1 Corinthians 11:10 where Paul said "It is for this reason that a woman [wife] ought to have authority over her own head, because of the angels," meaning authority *over* her marital head, the husband. In short, the wife has authority in the household, even over her husband. This reading is supported by the phasing of the verse in several translations, e.g. NIV, ISV, Douay-Rheims and Aramaic Bible in Plain English. Of course the more popular interpretation is that Paul was talking about a *symbol of* authority *on* her head; in other words, a head covering, aka hat. The problem with this reading is that the Greek word for "authority" just means authority or power and not "*a symbol of* authority" or "*a sign of* authority."

the years to come it became clear that he struggled with his relationship with the Lord and would fall out of fellowship for periods of time. I remained casual friends with him regardless and we'd discuss biblical topics now and then on the internet. Then, suddenly, he started going on curious rants publicly about how the devil wrote the Scriptures and so they're not a reliable source of truth, blah, blah, blah. I was hoping this was just a phase, but he has continued with this erroneous attitude for months now and has been very vocal about these grossly heretical beliefs. Carol & I couldn't help wonder how his godly wife was handling the situation. Obviously her husband's actions disqualified him of being a subordinate spiritual head in the marriage.

So Paul's goal — led of the Spirit — was for believers to have healthy marriages in Ephesus. He wanted wives to respect their husbands as the head of the marriage & family rather than treat them with contempt with an arrogant attitude bolstered by Artemis worship and Gnosticism. This was likewise the case in the Corinthian situation ten years prior, except that the negative influence there was Dionysian worship (and likely Gnosticism as well). Of course the apostle elsewhere stressed how husbands were to love their wives as Christ loved the Church and gave himself up for her. Paul's aim was to have healthy marriages & families in the church. It's a noble goal — a *good* thing, not a bad thing. When wives refuse to give their husbands the respect due them it'll naturally suck the life out of the husband and the marriage will eventually fall apart. I've unfortunately seen this happen with friends!

Honor the One Who Wears Your Ring

So, please, whether you're the husband or wife, *honor* **the one who wears your ring**. Honor & love him/her even when you see someone of the opposite sex that might attract you or shows a modicum of interest. Honor & love your spouse by not even giving your thought life over to dwelling on another person (Job 31:1, 31:9-10 & Matthew 5:28). Are you following? This doesn't mean you won't find certain people of the opposite sex attractive on occasion, it just means you honor your spouse & marriage by not daydreaming about them. For anyone who argues that a truly godly person wouldn't experience such a temptation in the first place, *wrong*. It happened to Job and he was the most righteous person on the face of the Earth at the time (Job 1:8). Why else do you think he made a "covenant with his eyes" so as not to look at a woman in the wrong spirit, both outer eye and inner eye (Job 31:1)?

By the way, when I suggest that spouses should honor the one who wears their ring, I don't mean that we should condone sin. Intercede for your spouse when you see sin issues, confront as led of the Spirit and forgive when s/he humbly repents (Luke 17:3-4). Furthermore, as clichéd as it may sound: **The family that prays together stays together.** Carol & I pray together on a daily basis. I encourage couples to do the same. It keeps you tight and in sync with God.

7

Understanding Women "According to Knowledge"

Moved by the Spirit, Peter instructed husbands to live with their wives "according to knowledge" (1 Peter 3:7).[9] Regardless of whether you're male or female, this is what this book is all about — helping you acquire knowledge and understanding of women via the God-breathed Scriptures rather than erroneous religion or secular philosophy. While this verse is technically referring to *husbands* living with their *wives* "according to knowledge," the principle is applicable to any woman in your life — a sister, a friend, a neighbor, a coworker, a supervisor, a boss.

We live in a peculiar age where Leftwing "leaders" and their bought "scientists" insist that there is zero difference between men and women. For a man to become a woman all he has to do is have his penis surgically removed and — *viola* — he instantaneously becomes a woman; that is, as long as he takes feminine hormones.

---

[9] The word for 'knowledge' in the Greek is a form of *gnosis (NOH-sis)*, which simply means "knowledge" or "understanding."

The problem with this, of course, is that his DNA would still be male. In other words, scientifically speaking, he would yet be a man regardless of the creative mutilation to his genitals and the unnatural hormonal treatments.

The Bible says that we should live with or relate to women "according to knowledge" and so in this closing chapter I'd like to stress some beneficial qualities unique to the feminine spirit. Some of these qualities we touched on in previous chapters while others will be new. Let's start with…

Women are to "Subdue" or "Govern" their part of the Earth

God gave the commission to subdue or govern the Earth to *both* Adam & Eve, not just Adam (man):

> **And God blessed <u>them</u>, and said unto <u>them</u>, "Be fruitful, and multiply, and replenish <u>the earth</u>, and <u>subdue it</u>: and <u>have dominion</u> over the fish of the sea, and over the fowl of the air, and over every living thing that moveth upon the earth."**
> **Genesis 1:28** (KJV)

This blessing/directive is inherent in the psycho-spiritual DNA of humankind — male *and* female. There's no escaping it; it's our Divine mission; it's part of who we *are*. Unfortunately, the sin nature inevitably twists this blessing and it becomes a curse, resulting in abuse, slavery, wars, environmental raping, etc. Yet, this doesn't take away from the fact that the intrinsic blessing is wholly *good* and was intended to *empower* humanity to fulfill its Divine mandate — to be fruitful, multiply, replenish, subdue and take dominion. In other words, the LORD didn't create humankind to be servants of the Earth, but to be lords over it, which is befitting since Father God is "Lord of heaven and earth," as Jesus Christ Himself acknowledged (Matthew 11:25). Keep in mind that humanity is created in God's image and believers are called to be "imitators of God" (Ephesians 5:1).

Before I go any further, I want to stress that the LORD doesn't want us to "subdue" and take "dominion" in a negative sense. I have to emphasize this since many people equate "dominion" with carnal control because the devil naturally tries to pervert whatever God creates, commands or blesses. The Creator's mandate was to subdue and hold dominion in LOVE, because "God is love" (1 John 4:7-8,16). This helps make sense of this proverb:

> **Love and faithfulness keep a king safe; through love his throne is made secure.**
> **Proverbs 20:28**

A "king" refers to an authority figure. In our day and age it would apply to anyone who has authority in any given environment: a father or mother, a teacher or professor, an employer or supervisor, a president or governor, a pastor or apostle, a police officer or security guard, etc. This proverb reveals the godly way of keeping one's position of authority — one's "throne" — safe and secure: **Through love and faithfulness.** So, when the Bible talks about "subduing" and taking "dominion" it's talking about doing so in love and faithfulness, not being an abusive tyrant. Are you with me?

David said "The boundary lines have fallen for me in pleasant places; surely I have a delightful inheritance" (Psalm 16:6). David's calling was to be a wise king of Israel; those were his "boundary lines" and they were indeed pleasant, but also very challenging at times, to say the least.

What's your assignment from the LORD? What are your boundary lines? What are you to "subdue" and "govern"? Answer: Your mind & thoughts, your body, your relationships, your marriage, your homestead, your animals, your job, the corresponding responsibilities and your service for God, which would include the way you can personally fulfill the Great Commission (Matthew 28:18-20). Keep in mind that the Great commission doesn't just involve sharing the awesome message of Christ and acquiring converts, but also discipling (training) believers to walk in newness of life by teaching them the rightly-divided Word of Truth and being a living epistle (2 Corinthians 3:2-3 & Matthew 5:13-16).

As for Carol & me, we have "subdued" our homestead on top of Howland Hill in northeast Ohio and we "hold dominion" over our ministry, Fountain of Life, whereupon we fulfill the Great Commission, reaching people all over the Earth on a daily basis.

A Woman is a "Helper" as God is a Helper

We observed in chapter **4** that women are to be the "helper" of their mate, which would naturally extend toward their children. We saw that that the Hebrew word translated as "helper" is *ezer (AY-zer)*, which is used once in the Bible in regards to women, but 16 times in reference to the LORD helping human beings. The root word is *azar (aw-ZAR)*, which means "to surround," "protect" or "aid" according to the Strong's lexicon. Thus women help their mates and those under their guardianship in the sense of surrounding, protecting and aiding them, just as God does with those who believe. We observe this in Deuteronomy 33:29 where it says that the LORD is Israel's "shield and helper (*ezer*) and your glorious sword." This obliterates the idea that women are merely to be servant girls, fetching coffee or what have you.

Another good example is this psalm:

> ¹I lift up my eyes to the mountains—
>   where does my <u>help</u> *(ezer)* come from?
> ²My <u>help</u> *(ezer)* comes from the LORD,
>   the Maker of heaven and earth.
> ³He will not let your foot slip—
>   he who <u>watches over you</u> will not slumber;
> ⁴indeed, he who <u>watches over</u> Israel
>   will neither slumber nor sleep.
> ⁵<u>The LORD watches over you</u>—
>   The LORD is your shade at your right hand;
> ⁶the sun will not harm you by day,
>   nor the moon by night.
> ⁷<u>The LORD will keep you from all harm</u>—
>   he will <u>watch over your life</u>;
> ⁸the LORD will <u>watch over your coming and going</u>
>   both now and forevermore.
>
> **Psalm 121**

Just as God helped the faithful Israelites in the sense of watching over them, so a woman is anointed of the LORD to help and watch over her mate and anyone under her care. Do all women actively do this? No, but that's usually because she's been abused somehow and this wonderful quality is submerged. Yet it can emerge (or reemerge) and be a blessing to people if the proverbial truth sets her free (John 8:31-32). This is one of the reasons this book exists.

As Proverbs 24:5 says, **a wise person has power** and **a man of knowledge increases strength**, which applies to *both* males and females. Do you want to walk in power and strength? Then make the effort to acquire wisdom and knowledge applicable to your situation, starting with mastering the powerful scriptural truths in this book!

A woman will surround & protect her man and those under her guardianship like a fierce mother bear with her cubs (Hosea 13:8). She'll keep her eye open to potential homewreckers and become a wall between her husband and the seductress or false accuser. She discerns bad character and protects her children from negative influences; her husband too (1 Corinthians 15:33 & Proverbs 13:20).

However, a wise, godly woman refuses to turn a blind eye to sin and foolishly defend the transgressor, even if it's her spouse or child. For instance, if a husband has a fleshly penchant for sloth, legalism, porn, arrogance or gossip/slander she won't condone it, but rather hold him accountable by correcting him via the God-breathed Scriptures (2 Timothy 3:16-17). This is a necessary form of love — *tough* love (Proverbs 27:5-6). My wife and I correct each other all the time. Why? Because we love each other.

Women have a Nurturing Spirit—they *Nourish* those assigned to Them

Females have the gift to *nurture* those within their sphere of influence, like their husbands, children and so forth. To nurture means "to nourish, feed; to foster growth." The Creator does it with birds (Matthew 6:26), Naomi did it with her grandson (Ruth 4:16) and Mary did it with the child Jesus (Luke 11:27).

Yes, males can nourish to a degree, but women are especially gifted in this area. For instance, a father can bottle-feed his infant, but he'll be looking at the clock the entire time whereas the mother carries the baby for 9 months (!) and, after birthing, enjoys the endeavor of bottle-feeding or breastfeeding, losing consciousness of time.

Notice in the Bible how the wife of noble character is obsessed with nourishing her husband & kids, as well as others, including her employees (if applicable) and the needy:

> [14]**She is like the merchant ships,**
>   **bringing her food from afar.**
> [15]**She gets up while it is still night;**
>   **she provides food for her family**
>   **and portions for her female servants.**
> [16]**She considers a field and buys it;**
>   **out of her earnings she plants a vineyard.**
> [17]**She sets about her work vigorously;**
>   **her arms are strong for her tasks.**
> [18]**She sees that her trading is profitable,**
>   **and her lamp does not go out at night.**
> [19]**In her hand she holds the distaff**
>   **and grasps the spindle with her fingers.**
> [20]**She opens her arms to the poor**
>   **and extends her hands to the needy.**
> **Proverbs 31:14-20**

This applies to spiritual food as well as physical food. Christ emphasized the importance of both (Matthew 4:4). While husbands will stay in a dead assembly until Jesus comes back, mothers will seek out healthy fellowships & ministries so that their families will be spiritually nourished and not famished. I attended an excellent mega-church for a decade as a young believer and I used to see solitary women come to check out the ministry, sometime on the mid-week services or Sunday nights. After a while the husband or kids would inevitably join her. What was the woman doing? She was searching for a healthy ministry that could properly nourish her family!

How Can these Wonderful Qualities Emerge?

Abuse always submerges a person's positive qualities. For instance, my father was a good provider and regularly took the family on outings, like camping, hiking, swimming and movies, but I had zero relationship with him. He constantly put me down and called me profane names for no ostensible reason except I guess it made him feel like a ruler. Hence, many of my attributes as a young man were squelched and submerged inside of me. I thankfully reconciled with the LORD when I was 20 years-old and so started coming near to my Creator. The Bible says that **if you come near to God then God will come near to you** (James 4:8). Since "God is love" (1 John 4:8,16), the closer I got to the LORD the more of God's love I experienced and it set me free, bringing out my submerged potential. It's like the warm rays of the sun making a dying plant grow and blossom.

This principle works for both masculine and feminine attributes. If you're a female, you can walk in the awesome assets noted in this chapter and others — perhaps you already are to some degree — but it's going to take love to draw them out in increasing measure if they're submerged for one reason or another. Abuse and hatred are life-stifling and growth-stultifying while love is life-giving. "God *is* the fountain of life" (Psalm 36:9) so make the effort to come near to the LORD on a regular basis by:

1. Cultivating a 24/7 prayer life (1 Thessalonians 5:17),
2. Feeding from God's Word (Matthew 4:4),
3. Regularly hooking up with other believers from healthy assemblies (Proverbs 13:20), and
4. Feeding from anointed fivefold ministers (Ephesians 4:11-13).

Put into practice what you learn, change your thinking accordingly, which is what "renewing the mind" means (Romans 12:1-2), and develop a persevering spirit. Life's a fight, *fight it!* As you come near to God and vice versa you'll increase in God's favor (2 Peter 3:18)[10] and your attributes will manifest more and more.

Males can help the ladies in their lives manifest their natural attributes by loving them, whether wives, girlfriends, daughters or friends. Husbands are to love their wives "just as Christ loved the church and gave himself up for her to make her holy, cleansing her by the washing with water through the word" (Ephesians 5:25-26). The Greek word for love in this verse is *agapé (uh-GAH-pay)*, which is defined in 1 Corinthians 13:4-7. It refers to practical love rather than merely a feeling; it's **love-in-action**. Practicing this kind of love *counteracts* the curse of Genesis 3:16.

Men are to love their women "*just as* Christ loved the church," which illustrates that:

1. Men are to be the *initiator* of love.
2. Men are to love the woman **right where she currently is** (which doesn't mean condoning sin).
3. Men are to put the woman *first*, above themselves.

The Lord did all these things for his bride, the church, and so men are to do likewise with their women, especially if they want them to be a blessing in their lives, i.e. the ideal "Proverbs 31 woman."

---

[10] I'm not talking about God's grace for salvation here, which is received simply through repentance & faith (Acts 20:21 & Mark 1:15), but rather God's grace — *favor* — in your personal life. For example, Jesus **grew in favor** with the Father when he was on Earth (Luke 2:40,52). Samuel did the same thing in the Old Testament (1 Samuel 2:26). For details, see my book *GRACE: What is It? How Do You Grow in It?* (2020).

But, if you're a woman, you don't need any man to love you in order to walk in your God-given attributes. Draw near to the LORD, as detailed above, and the LORD will draw near to you, which means you'll walk in God's favor (James 4:8). You don't need to be in an ideal situation in order to function in Divine grace and be blessed! For instance, Joseph was a type of Christ and he was *a slave* in Potiphar's house and *a prisoner* in Egypt, but the Bible says he prospered in both undesirable environments despite the obvious limitations thereof because the LORD was with him and blessed him (Genesis 39:2-6 & 39:20-23).

These are liberating truths! They reveal that no child of God has to identify as a perpetual victim and live their life according to victimhood idiotology. Instead, you move forward in bold faith despite the challenging situations, walking in Divine favor and fulfilling the LORD's will, bearing fruit in every good work (Colossians 1:10). Amen!

Be Careful NOT to put all Men, Women and Marriages in a Box

Allow me to close by stressing that we have to be careful *not* to put people — either gender — in a box; marriages too. For instance, Jacob was renamed Israel and became the progenitor of God's nation on Earth, but he was a Momma's boy who favored hanging around the tents; meanwhile his half-brother, Esau, was a hairy manly man who preferred the outdoors and hunting (Genesis 25:27, 27:11 & 27:22-23). In short, Jacob was stereotypically Liberal whereas Esau was stereotypically Rightwing. Obviously God had no problem using a so-called "Momma's boy" as an instrumental figure in the divine plan for redemption.

In the New Testament Christ reveals his loving gentleness at times (Matthew 11:29) — a supposedly Liberal trait — while at others he was a veritable holy terror (Mark 11:15-18). As Solomon said, "It is good to grasp the one and not let go of the other. Whoever fears God will avoid all **extremes**" (Ecclesiastes 7:16-18). Meanwhile the Lord pointed out the glaring contrasts of those who live off the grid in the wilderness, like John the Baptist who wore garments made of camel hair and ate locusts & wild honey, contrasted by those who live in palaces, wearing fine apparel and dining on exquisite cuisines (Matthew 3:1-6 & 11:7-8).

Regarding women, the Bible features the all-encompassing national leadership of Deborah as well as the meek purity of Mother Mary. Then there's Jael who had no qualms about smashing a tent peg through the temple of a Canaanite commander. Meanwhile sisters Martha & Mary were like night and day.

As far as marriages go, they all feature different dynamics based on two unique people and their corresponding social stratum. In today's society, women aren't necessarily preoccupied with raising kids for about 30 years from the start of their early marriages, as was the case in biblical times. They may likely work outside the home and have careers while husbands may have unconventional occupations, working from or at the home.

Allow Christian couples to make their own decisions about these matters and who does what or why, working within scriptural guidelines as led of the Holy Spirit. Don't nose into other people's business. How God works in other believers' lives is none of our concern; our concern is to follow the Lord and fulfill the responsibilities of our distinctive callings (John 21:21-22).

Paul expressed it perfectly when he asked, "Who are you to judge someone else's servant?" (Romans 14:4). He was referring to judging other believers on any type of disputable matter, like what food to eat and what holiday to celebrate. By stressing "<u>someone else's</u> servant," Paul meant *God's* servant, that is, **other believers**. Simply put, other believers are God's servant, not your servant or my servant. Even in cases where a believer functions within a pastor's "flock," the pastor is merely the under-shepherd, not the Chief Shepherd; Christ is the Chief Shepherd (1 Peter 5:1-4). This is why the text instructs pastors to not lord it over believers, but rather be humble, godly examples (if they can't do that then they have no business being pastors).

<u>Closing Word</u>

I hope you were blessed by this study and that the scriptural truths have increased your understanding of women from a biblical perspective and women functioning in God's service, as well as the dynamics of husband & wife in marriage. I also trust you have a more balanced understanding of those "hard sayings" on women in the church.

May the LORD bless you in your service as you continually draw closer to God, seek the truth and apply what you've learned.

Amen.

Bibliography

Brown, Francis/Driver, S.R./Briggs, Charles A. *Brown-Driver-Briggs Lexicon.* Peabody: Hendrickson Publishers, 1994

Cameneti, Joseph. *The Uniqueness of a Woman, Parts II & III* (series). Believers Christian Fellowship, Warren, OH. 1994

Helps Word-Studies Lexicon. Retrieved from Biblehub.com. 1987, 2011

Hinkley, Chesna. *What to Say When Someone Says that Patriarchy is God's Plan.* Retrieved from https://www.cbeinternational.org/resource/article/mutuality-blog-magazine/what-say-when-someone-says-patriarchy-gods-plan, 2019

Kirkwood, David. *Your Best Year Yet!* Pittsburgh: Ethnos Press, 1996

Kroeger, Richard & Catherine Clark Kroeger. *Pandemonium and Silence at Corinth.* Retrieved from https://www.cbeinternational.org/resource/article/pandemonium-and-silence-corinth, 1978

LORD, The. *English Standard Version (ESV). Holy Bible.* Chicago: Crossway, 2001

LORD, The. *King James Version. Holy Bible.* Iowa Falls: World Bible Publishers

LORD, The. *New International Version (Revised). Holy Bible.* Nashville: Holman, 2011

LORD, The. *New King James Version Study Bible: Second Edition.* Nashville: Thomas Nelson, 2012

LORD, The. *New Revised Standard Version. Holy Bible.* Nashville: Nelson, 1989

LORD, The. *The Amplified Bible.* Grand Rapids: Zondervan, 1987

LORD, The. *Quest Study Bible: New International Version.* Grand Rapids: Zondervan, 2003

Servant, David. *Heaven Word Daily.* Pittsburgh: Ethnos Press, 2009

Strong, James. *Strong's Exhaustive Concordance.* Grand Rapids: Baker, 1991

Vine, W.E. *Vine's Expository Dictionary of Biblical Words.* Cambridge: Nelson, 1985

Fountain of Life

Teaching Ministry

(Psalm 36:9)

The mission of Fountain of Life is to **set the captives FREE** by **reaching the world** with the **life-changing truths of God's Word**, the **power of the Holy Spirit** and the **Awesome News of the message of Jesus Christ**.

We're calling Spiritual Warriors all over the Earth to partner with us on this mission!

Books by Dirk Waren:

The Believer's Guide to FORGIVENESS & WARFARE
Legalism Unmasked
HELL KNOW! (full and condensed versions)
SHEOL KNOW! (full and condensed versions)
The Four Stages of Spiritual Growth
ANGELS: Their Purpose and Your Responsibility
THE LAW and the Believer
The SIX BASIC DOCTRINES of Christianity
GRACE: What is It? How Do You Grow in It?
How to Handle OFFENSES: Personal & Criminal
WOMEN in Ministry ...in God's Service

www.ingramcontent.com/pod-product-compliance
Lightning Source LLC
Chambersburg PA
CBHW070534030426
42337CB00016B/2194